# ISSUES IN ETHICS AND APPLIED ETHICS SERIES

VOLUME X

# Ethics of Values and Education

*Issues in Ethics and Applied Ethics Series*

Vol. 1. Ethics in Business, Applied and Environment
Vol. 2. Ethics in Feminism
Vol. 3. Socio-political Ethics
Vol. 4. Biomedical Ethics (Part I);
Biomedical Ethics (Part II)
Vol. 5. Metaethics (Part I); Normative Ethics and Virtue Ethics (Part II)
Vol. 6. Ethics of Business and Economics (Forthcoming)
Vol. 7. Ethics in Cārvāka/Lokāyata; Morality and Secularism (Forthcoming)
Vol. 8. Philosophy and Ethics of the Jainism (Forthcoming)
Vol. 9. Philosophy and Ethics of the Buddhism (Forthcoming)
Vol. 10. Ethics of Values and Education

---

**About the Editors**

**Shiva Nath Prasad**, after completing his studies, served Bihar government in several capacities. After retirement he became a full timer in the pursuit of philosophy. He edited a bilingual journal *Abhranta* later edited two journals separately one in English namely *Journal of Bihar Philosophical Research* and *Darshan Digdarshan* in Hindi. He authored one book *Charvaka/Lokayata Analytical* and *Hermeneutics Study*, a very unique book, which is a "singular attempt to reconstruct this almost a vanished system of India". He also published an Anthology namely *Phenomenology: Methodological Introduction* with Professor V.T. Sebastian of Panjab University. His multi-volume Anthology on Ethics and Applied Ethics (more than fifteen volumes) are being published by Concept Publishing Company Pvt. Ltd. and some are being processed. His latest book just published is *Reflections on Charvaka/Lokayata: The Gita and Rajneesh*. The author has to his Current about thirty published books and many are still in process of publications.

**Dr Avinash Kumar Srivastava**, born in December 1955 in Singthu village, Nalanda District, Bihar, holds a master's degree in philosophy from Patna University and earned his Ph.D. from Magadha University, Bodh Gaya. His doctoral research focused on *"A Comparative Study of Samadhi (Yoga) in Early Buddhism and the Bhagavad Gita."*

He began his academic career in March 1981 at J.J. College, Jhumri Telaiya (under Ranchi University), and later joined Nalanda College, Bihar Sharif, in August 1982. He retired as a Professor of Philosophy from Patliputra University.

A prolific scholar and writer, Dr Srivastava has authored two books—*Living Buddhism* and *Bharatiya Darshan Ki Mool Samasyayen*—and edited eleven anthologies. He has published around one hundred research papers in national and international journals.

Dr Srivastava is widely recognized in academic circles across India. He has served in several key roles, including Joint Secretary and Secretary of the Akhil Bharatiya Darshan Parishad, General Secretary of the Bihar Darshan Parishad, and Vice-President of the Indian Society for Buddhist Studies. He has also been a member of the editorial boards of *Buddha Prajna Sindhu, Ocean of Buddhist Wisdom* (Delhi), and *Darshnik Traimasik* of the Akhil Bharatiya Darshan Parishad.

# ISSUES IN ETHICS AND APPLIED ETHICS SERIES

## VOLUME X

# Ethics of Values and Education

*Edited by*

Shiva Nath Prasad
Avinash Kumar Srivastava

CONCEPT PUBLISHING COMPANY PVT. LTD.
NEW DELHI - 110 059

**ISBN:** 978-81-8069-976-4 (Series)
**ISBN:** 978-93-6344-922-0 (Vol. 10)

First Published 2026

*Published and Printed by*

Concept Since 1974

**Concept Publishing Company Pvt. Ltd.**
A/15-16, Commercial Block, Mohan Garden
New Delhi-110059 (India)
*T*: +91-11-41101460
*E*: publishing@conceptpub.com, *W*: www.conceptpub.com

**Cataloging in Publication**--Courtesy: D.K. Agencies (P) Ltd. <docinfo@dkagencies.com>

**Ethics of values and education /** edited by Shiva Nath Prasad, Avinash Kumar Srivastava.
pages cm. -- (Issues in ethics and applied ethics series ; volume X)
Contributed articles.
Includes bibliographical references.
ISBN 9788180699764 (series)
ISBN 9789363449220 (vol. 10)

1. Moral education--India. 2. Values--Study and teaching--India. 3. Education--India. I. Prasad, Shiva Nath, editor. II. Śrīvāstava, Avināsh Kumar, 1955- editor. III. Series: Issues in ethics and applied ethics series ; volume X.

LCC LC315.I4E84 2026 | DDC 370.1140954 23

# Foreword

This book entitled *Ethics of Values and Education* is tenth of "Issues in Ethics and Applied Ethics Series". This comprises, twenty two essays, written by Indian scholars, who have streamlined, the problems of education prevailing in India. The essence of this issue is "value education". The first essay has been written by Professor R.C. Sinha, which pinpoint an important feature of educational development in India. He has mentioned Sri Aurobindo, who envisaged "A National System of Education". Education is not mere learning, but it is cultivation of values. Professor Sinha subscribes to Gandhian philosophy of education and contemplates, that new education policy of the present government, is deeply concerned with character-building and value education of children. The second essay entitled, "Some Philosophical Reflections on the Moral Value Education" by Professor Jagat Pal, which elucidates the programme of moral education at school level. He asserts that the role of our moral education and school, should always be only to propose certain moral values to students in a rational manner, but not to impose anything on students. The creativity needs freedom. While imparting moral value, school must adopt rational approach. Value can be inculcated but not imposed. Value education helps students to develop good disposition that enables them to develop intellectually, socially and morally. Professor Jagat Pal rightly observes that the programme of character education does not, thus, simply mean a lesson, or course on moral values. The third article is written by Professor Avinash Kumar Srivastava, who is one of the editors of this book. His article bears the title "Rise of Education System and Its Moral Values". He upholds, that education plays dominant role in shaping, the child's mind-behaviour. He maintains primitive education has not been progressive but imitative. The fourth article is entitled "Role of Education in Cultivation of Values" by Dhanpat Raj Bhandari. He holds that education for learning and cultivation of values can be provided to students directly, or indirectly. He adheres, that education can achieve its ultimate purpose of making one, an ideal human being. The sixth article titled "Private, 'Public' Schools and the Right to Education" by Sri Mahi Pal Singh, dwells upon the aspect of education in our country. He urges that government school should be strengthened. The private school is producing snobs who feel superior in comparison with those of poor class students reading in government school. This is the stark reality, which he has streamlined. The seventh essay on "Plight of Government Schools: Who is Responsible?" by Sri Mahi Pal Singh is an eye-opener, since he has stressed on the shortcomings of government schools. D.R. Bhandari in his paper titled "Gandhian Thought and Modern Indian Education" upholds that there are some modern social thinkers, who accept that this sort of education provides for an all round development of the individual. The head, heart, and hand, all the three should be harmoniously developed. In the chapter nine, Professor Y.V. Satyanarayana dwells on "Philosophy and Education: The Indian Perspectives". He says that education is essential ingredient of life. It is education, that makes a distinction between a man and a beast. Educational philosophy plays a vital role in creation of good persons and a new social order. It is an efficient instrument for social change. Dr Abha Singh in her article "Dimensions of Education: A Gandhian Perspective" upholds that education is life-long process of learning. Gandhi devised his views on education in traditional Indian pattern, but she accepted new ideas of modern life. She holds correctly, that English education in India exposed our people to the technological developments, which were sweeping in the West. But exclusive English education is devoid of value-content, spoils human personality. In the paper titled "Value Education: A Critical Appraisal." by Professor Sarita Kumari emphasizes on value education, which aims at the maximum development in the direction of total upliftment of man and society. Professor Yamini Sahay in the chapter twelve writes on "Ethical Issues in Higher Education", that the call for university, to take ethics seriously is not new. She adhered that moral development must be considered an integral part of the education. Professor Sahay holds that college and university must have obligation to contribute to the moral development of students. Professor Kumkum Sinha in her article "Education and Swami Vivekananda: A Quest of life" explains, the meaning of education. According to Vivekananda, education means unfoldment of knowledge, which in inherent in man in the present age. Moral and religious values are being undermined. Education must have mission of man-making and character-building. The man-making for Vivekananda means a harmonious development of the body, mind and soul. Again, in thirteenth chapter "Education and Globalization: A Philosophical Study" of the present book, Dr Kumkum Sinha makes an attempt to a philosophical study of the problem of education and globalization. Globalization has changed the native quality of the world. Our educational institutions are producing global citizens who can work in a borderless economy and live in a global society. The fifteenth essay is captioned "Education, Ethics and Values" by Rajjan Kumar and Sunita Kumari. The authors say that education is a process of acquisition and transmission of knowledge. Education is a preparation of life. Ethics is a system of code of morals; values do not mean only virtues. Moral values are known as virtues. Professor D.C. Srivastava in his article entitled "Buddhist Ethics and Education" writes that education can be understood as self-correction through self-realization. The objection of Buddhist education is to pull out the potential in each person. The education according to Buddha is cultivation of values like *prajñā*, *śīla*, and *samādhi*. Buddhist education shows us how to act ethically with wisdom and mindfulness. In the seventeenth chapter, Sohan Raj Tater writes about value education. He refers to a very significant book written by Samuel P. Huntington titled *The Clash of Civilization and Remaking of the World Order*. Huntington urges that the problem of decline of culture in the west is quite appealing. The Christian view is that man is born sinner. Vedāntic view is, that man is born divine. Value education is going to emerge as a new science. The challenges in front of today's techno-globalism, is the creation of value-based human beings. In another article, Dr Tater contemplates the "Need of Value Education in Modern Era". That transmission of knowledge is possible through technology. Education is one of the principal means available to man. Education is the only hope for the future. Value education responds to the challenges of twenty-first century. In recent past, we find that teaching of different religions are gaining momentum. The interfaith education is to create a culture of peace. In twentieth chapter of the book, Dr Archana Srivastava writes on "Creating the Ecologically Responsible Culture" that there is need for thinking about environmental ethics. The article entitled "Evaluation in Teacher Education is a Tool for Quality Sustainability" by Shashirekha S.M. attempts to state that evaluation is going. The teacher is the most important element in any educational programme. It is the teacher who is responsible for implementation of educational plans and process at any stage.

This book presents twenty-second chapter titled "Philosophy Education and Ethics/Values or Axiology" by

Sri Shiva Nath Prasad. The editor considers that this book covers some of the issues of the philosophy of education. Sri Shiva Nath Prasad is a passionate reader and prolife writer on philosophical issues. In this chapter, he has mentioned the book entitled *Four Philosophies* written by J.D. Butler. Professor Butler says that it is difficult to define the word "Education". But Butler holds that philosophy is most indispensable for life. Philosophy is theoretical and education is practical. The actual process of education is a matter of practice. Philosophy gives world view. Sri Shiva Nath Prasad upholds that theorizing merely cannot assure any result without practice. Theory without practice is a half-way process. Both theory and practice are essential.

I thank editors for taking great pains to edit valuable titles on value education. I hope this collection of philosophy of education will be helpful to students and teachers as well.

*25 August 2025*

**R.C. Sinha**
National Fellow
Indian Institute of Advanced Study
Shimla

# Preface

This volume, *Ethics of Values and Education*, part of the esteemed "Issues in Ethics and Applied Ethics Series", aims to illuminate the purpose and function of education, and its profound influence on human development from early childhood, even when seemingly limited to teaching. It delves into complex and challenging topics such as the evolution, dimensions, and value of educational systems, its dimensions, value, and systematic development of man and society.

A closer look at education reveals its many facets and meanings, with differing views on its ultimate purpose and practical application. It's far from a single concept; it holds many meanings and sparks varied perspectives on its aims and how it's carried out. Simply put, education is how we gain knowledge, master skills, and internalize values and attitudes through a range of learning experiences. This process can occur in various settings, including formal institutions like schools and universities, non-formal environments such as workshops and community programmes, and informally through daily life experiences and social interactions.

The compilation of twenty-two essays in this anthology is valuable for everyone, as these give the key to a smooth living, surpassing and solving all the complex problems of human life. It achieves this by fostering academic insights and evolving values and virtues in both personal and social life. Education plays a crucial role in this process, especially value education, which instils social, ethical, and normative principles in individuals. It fosters character development and promotes one to evolve as a responsible citizen. By embedding virtues like honesty, integrity, and empathy, and developing a strong sense of right and wrong, this approach is vital for shaping well-rounded individuals. By embedding virtues like honesty, integrity, and empathy, and developing a strong sense of right and wrong, this approach is vital for shaping well-rounded individuals. It also encourages social responsibility, fosters emotional intelligence, and creates a positive learning environment all contributing to promoting holistic development with a moral compass. Thus, ethics has an important role in education as it provides a discipline dealing with good and bad with commitment and moral duty. Since education is the fundamental principle of human life, ethics becomes a pertinent principle here.

A global consensus among educationists highlights the necessity of a normative transformation in the entire education system. This comes from the understanding that humans are dynamic, ever-evolving beings, continuously advancing through various developmental stages. But, for the proper development in the right direction, value-centric education, moral education is needed. Indian seers understood and have said much earlier than Western civilization that "education provides humility in behaviour" (*vidyā dadāti vinayam, vinayam dadāti pātratām*). This volume, *Ethics of Values and Education*, directly addresses this critical need.

**Shiva Nath Prasad**
**Avinash Kumar Srivastava**

# Acknowledgements

The present volume, *Ethics of Values and Education*, a part of the "Ethics and Applied Ethics Series", seeks to explore the multifaceted and distinctive perspectives of education—its intrinsic values and the essential role of ethics within it. Education profoundly shapes the outlook of students and, by extension, the character of society. When normative principles and human values are instilled from early childhood through the learning years, they lay the foundation for an ideal society.

Our own perspectives have been shaped by numerous influences—parents, teachers, classmates, books, and many others. In compiling this volume, we have drawn inspiration, assistance, and contributions from a number of esteemed authors whose scholarly works enrich these pages. Their names are too numerous to list, but we extend our heartfelt thanks to all our mentors, friends, and well-wishers for their continued support over the years.

Above all, we owe a deep debt of gratitude to all those, both directly and indirectly, who have made this publication possible.

We extend our heartfelt gratitude to all the contributors of this volume for their scholarly articles. This work has been a long-standing endeavour, yet the unforeseen challenges brought about by the COVID-19 pandemic caused significant setbacks, halting progress for a considerable period. During this time, we received numerous inquiries from contributors concerning the status of their submissions. We sincerely apologize for the inordinate delay and deeply regret any inconvenience it may have caused.

Our hearts are especially heavy for those esteemed contributors who, sadly, are no longer with us. We feel a profound sense of remorse and bear the weight of not having been able to bring their work to publication sooner.

We extend our sincere gratitude to Professor R.C. Sinha, who not only contributed a scholarly article to this volume but also graciously penned its Foreword. Our heartfelt thanks also go to all the contributors whose insightful writings have enriched these pages.

We are deeply indebted to the members of our families, whose understanding and sacrifices in their daily lives have supported our academic pursuits. We wish to make special mention of Raghvendra, son of Sri Shivanath Prasad, whose unwavering dedication and exceptional contribution have played a pivotal role in the publication of this book series.

We also express our appreciation to Sri A.K. Mittal, Proprietor of Concept Publishing Company Pvt. Ltd., for his personal interest and commitment in reviving the publication of the series in general, and this volume in particular.

**Shiva Nath Prasad**
**Avinash Kumar Srivastava**

# Contents

# List of Contributors

**Abha Singh,** Professor & Head, P.G. Department of Philosophy, Patliputra University, Patna. Residence: 203, Jaikunj, Apartment, Kidwaipuri, Patna, Bihar.

**Archana Srivastava,** Professor and Head, Department of Economics, JDVM P.G. College, Kanpur. Residence: 117/Q/10 L.I.C. Colony, Sharda Nagar, Kanpur, Uttar Pradesh.

**Avinash Kumar Srivastava,** Former Professor of Philosophy, Patliputra University, Patna. Residence: 205, Guldawadi Apartment, Indrapuri, Road No. 10, Kesari Nagar Post Office, Near Puja Medicals, Patna, Bihar.
**Email:** avinash.srivastava39@gmail.com

**D.C. Srivastava,** Retired Professor of Philosophy, Christ Church College, Kanpur. Residence: 117/Q/10 L.I.C. Colony, Sharda Nagar, Kanpur, Uttar Pradesh.
**Email:** srivastava.dcsri@gmail.com

**D.R. Bhandari,** Former Professor of Philosophy, Jodhpur University, Rajasthan. Residence: C/o, Flat No. 302, Samriddhi, MDI, Gurgaon, Haryana.

**Jagat Pal,** Retired Professor, Residence: 176 A/F 01, Swastik Apartment, Tagore Town, Allahabad, Uttar Pradesh.

**Kumkum Sinha,** Head, Department of Philosophy, Jagjeewan College, Gaya. Residence: MIG-148, Adityapur-2, Jamshedpur, Jharkhand.

**Mahi Pal Singh,** Raghav Vihar, Phase 3, Prem Nagar, Dehradun, Uttarakhand.

**R.C. Sinha,** Former Chairperson, Indian Council of Philosophical Research. Residence: 201-202 Saptarshi Apartment, Rajkumari Complex, Kankarbagh (Near Bahadurpur Gumati), Patna, Bihar.
**Email:** rcsinha22@gmail.com

**Rajjan Kumar,** Ex-Head and Dean, Faculty of Education and Allied Science, M.J.P. Rohilkhand University, Bareilly, Uttar Pradesh.
**Email:** rajjanphil@gmail.com

**Sarita Kumari,** Head, P.G. Department of Philosophy (Retired), N.P. University Medininagar, Palamau, Daltongunj, Jharkhand. Residence: 205 Guldawadi Apartment, Indrapuri, Road No. 10, Kesari Nagar Post Office, Near Puja Medicals, Patna, Bihar.
**Email:** sarita.kumari1958nov@gmail.com

**Shashirekha S.M.** C/o 205 Guldawadi Apartment, Indrapuri, Road No. 10, Kesari Nagar Post Office, Near Puja Medicals, Patna, Bihar.

**Sohan Raj Tater,** 504 Riddhi Apartment, PAIIMS, Pal Road, Jodhpur, Rajasthan.
**Email:** sohan.tater@gmail.com

**Sunita Kumari,** Department of Sanskrit, BSM PG College Campus, Roorkee, Uttarakhand.

**Yamini Sahay,** Professor & Head, P.G. Department of Philosophy, Vinoba Bhave University, Hajaribagh, Jharkhand.
**Email:** sahay.yamini@gmail.com

**Y.V. Satyanarayana,** Former Professor of Philosophy, Andhra University (A.P). Residence: Door No. 45-16, Vidyanagar, Vishakhapatnam, Andhra Pradesh.
**Email:** satyanarayana48@gmail.com

# Introduction

Throughout the trajectory of human civilization, the definition, significance, and function of education have been subject to continuous evolution, shaped by dynamic socio-cultural contexts, historical contingencies, and shifting societal imperatives. Education theory recognizes that while pedagogical models and epistemological frameworks have varied across time and place, a foundational constant persists: the capacity of education to positively influence human development. This influence remains evident even when education is narrowly conceptualized as the transmission of information or knowledge to learners, highlighting its enduring role as a catalyst for individual growth and societal advancement. Such constancy underscores the theoretical assertion that education, in all its forms, serves as a fundamental mechanism for human flourishing. In the discourse of educational theory, the scope and impact of education have been interpreted through various philosophical lenses. John Stuart Mill offers one of the most comprehensive conceptualizations, positing that education encompasses not only intentional efforts—whether self-directed or externally administered—to cultivate human potential, but also the indirect influences that shape character and intellectual faculties. Mill's framework extends the boundaries of education to include the formative effects of institutions such as law, government, and industry, as well as environmental and social conditions like climate, geography, and cultural norms. This expansive view underscores the theoretical assertion that education is not confined to formal instruction but is a pervasive force embedded within the broader socio-political and ecological context, continuously contributing to the refinement of human nature. In his 1867 Rectorial Address at the University of St. Andrews, John Stuart Mill initially offered an expansive definition of education, encompassing all influences—intentional or incidental—that contribute to the development of human nature. However, recognizing the breadth of this interpretation, Mill subsequently proposed a more focused definition within the same address. He described education as "the culture which each generation purposely gives to those who are to be its successors to qualify them for at least maintaining, if possible, or improving the level of progress achieved". Both formulations, despite their differing scopes, converge on a central theoretical premise: education functions as a deliberate and continuous process aimed at human improvement and societal advancement. This dual perspective reflects a foundational tension in educational theory between broad sociocultural influences and structured pedagogical intent.

Beyond the foundational notion of education as a vehicle for human development, educational theory also recognizes two additional dimensions: education as a system of knowledge and as a form of cultural transmission. These dimensions highlight the notion that education is not limited to structured instruction or explicit pedagogical intent. For instance, a child acquires education through the lived experience of daily life, often in the absence of a defined curriculum, predetermined goals, or formal systems. Nevertheless, this informal process makes a meaningful contribution to shaping the individual, gradually modifying and developing cognitive and social faculties. Over time, such experiential learning becomes increasingly structured, incorporating systematic methods of knowledge dissemination aimed at fostering intellectual growth and cultural continuity. This duality between informal experience and formal instruction reflects the complex and layered nature of educational processes.

Within the broader discourse on education, development emerges as a central and unifying concept, with other dimensions of educational practice and theory often structured around it. This notion of development is intrinsically linked to the metaphor of the organism, suggesting that true development follows an inherent, organic law—unlike mechanical systems, which do not evolve autonomously. From this perspective, development is not merely the result of quantitative changes such as accretion or multiplication; rather, it is characterized by increasing structural complexity in conjunction with functional adaptation. This process of differentiation aligned with purposeful adaptation constitutes authentic development. Furthermore, a third and essential element—self-determination—is implicit in the organismic model. It posits that development originates, unfolds, and ultimately declines according to the internal principles governing the organism itself. In educational theory, this underscores the importance of fostering environments that support autonomous growth, recognizing the learner as an active, self-regulating participant in their own developmental trajectory.

While development remains a central theme in educational theory, it does not encompass the full complexity of the concept. A review of diverse definitions offered by eminent scholars reveals that education is inherently multifaceted, encompassing a range of interpretations that reflect varying philosophical, cultural, and pedagogical perspectives. At its core, education is understood as a dynamic process through which individuals acquire knowledge, skills, values, and attitudes—often shaped by both formal instruction and lived experience. This duality highlights that education is not merely a structured endeavour with predefined goals, but also an organic process of cultural transmission and personal growth, influenced by the broader social and experiential context in which learning occurs. The process of education unfolds across a variety of contexts, encompassing both formal institutional settings—such as schools, colleges, and universities—and informal environments, including workshops, everyday experiences, and social interactions. Educational theory acknowledges that the meaning of education extends beyond its literal definition, encompassing a range of implicit associations shaped by cultural, situational, and individual perspectives. This contextual variability underscores the complexity of education as a concept, revealing its capacity to function simultaneously as a structured system of knowledge transmission and as an organic process of personal and social development. The foundational components of education—namely the curriculum, learning environment, assessment mechanisms, educational objectives, and the learner—operate in an integrated manner to facilitate meaningful learning and holistic development. These elements collectively support the acquisition of knowledge, the cultivation of skills, and the nurturing of personal growth. At its core, education embodies the principles of intellectual and personal development, serving as a transformative process through which individuals unfold their inherent potential and acquire new capabilities. In this sense, education functions as a powerful instrument of empowerment, enabling individuals to enhance their quality of life, access new opportunities, and navigate their personal and professional trajectories with greater agency and purpose. Education is deeply intertwined with broader societal goals such as social progress, equity, and civic engagement. It serves not only as a mechanism for intellectual and personal development but also as a means of cultivating moral values, ethical principles, and socially responsible behaviour. Through its capacity to foster tolerance and active citizenship, education contributes to the formation of cohesive and inclusive societies. Importantly, the meaning and purpose of education are not universally fixed; they vary significantly across cultural and societal contexts, reflecting distinct values, priorities, and historical experiences. For instance, in some societies, education may be closely aligned with the promotion of religious faith and spiritual development, while in others, it may prioritize scientific inquiry, technological advancement, or the preservation of cultural heritage. This diversity underscores the need for educational theory to remain sensitive to contextual variations, recognizing education as a culturally embedded and ideologically nuanced phenomenon.

Given that the foundational principles of education—and the thematic focus of this discourse—include values and ethics, it is essential to examine their role within educational theory. Value education refers to the intentional process of imparting social, moral, and normative principles to learners, aiming to foster character development and cultivate responsible citizenship. Through structured and experiential learning, virtues such as honesty, integrity, empathy, and respect are embedded within the educational experience. This process not only nurtures a sense of ethical discernment—enabling learners to distinguish between right and wrong—but also contributes to the holistic development of personality. Moreover, value-based education promotes emotional intelligence, social responsibility, and a positive learning environment, all of which are integral to shaping a morally grounded and socially conscious individual. It is important to recognize, however, that the interpretation and emphasis of value education vary across cultural and societal contexts. While some societies may prioritize religious or spiritual dimensions, others may focus on scientific inquiry, civic responsibility, or the preservation of cultural heritage, reflecting diverse educational priorities and ethical frameworks.

As a foundational dimension of human life, education is inherently intertwined with ethical considerations. In contemporary educational contexts, the integration of technology has significantly expanded access to knowledge, yet it has also introduced complex ethical challenges—such as issues of academic integrity, including plagiarism and misuse of digital resources. These developments underscore the necessity of embedding ethics within the educational framework, not merely as an implicit value but as a distinct area of study. To appreciate the role of ethics in education, it is essential to first clarify its conceptual foundations. Ethics, derived from the Greek term ethos, meaning custom or character, is a central and active branch of philosophy concerned with moral reasoning and human conduct. It encompasses the values and virtues that inform our decisions and behaviours in everyday life. Within educational theory, ethics serves as a guiding principle for cultivating responsible, reflective, and socially conscious individuals. By incorporating ethical education into curricula, institutions can foster moral development, promote emotional intelligence, and create learning environments that support holistic growth and civic responsibility.

Ethics occupies a vital role within the educational system, serving as a foundational framework that ensures the smooth functioning of academic institutions and the protection of the rights and responsibilities of both educators and learners. By establishing clear standards of acceptable conduct, educational ethics safeguard the integrity of teaching and learning processes. In recent years, the significance of ethics in education has gained considerable attention, prompting institutions to introduce dedicated courses aimed at fostering ethical awareness among students. Ethical principles are not only accessible to learners but are also integral to the professional responsibilities of educators. In both day and residential schools across India, teachers are expected to instil ethical values in students, while school administrations often take proactive measures to familiarize educators with the ethical standards governing their profession. This institutional emphasis reflects a broader philosophical understanding of ethics—derived from the Greek term ethos, meaning custom or character—as a branch of philosophy concerned with moral values and human behaviour. Within the educational context, ethics guides actions and decisions, shaping the moral compass of individuals and contributing to the cultivation of a responsible and reflective citizenry.

Education is widely recognized as a fundamental human right, and within this framework, the role of ethics in education extends far beyond theoretical inquiry. The purpose of ethics education is not merely to study moral philosophy in abstraction, but to apply ethical reasoning to real-world contexts. It serves two primary objectives. First, it aims to cultivate the cognitive capacities necessary for individuals to identify and critically engage with ethical dimensions across diverse domains such as economics, public policy, medicine, and education itself. Second, ethics education fosters the development of critical thinking skills, particularly the ability to reflect on one's motivations and to evaluate the theoretical and practical consequences of individual and collective actions. This reflective capacity enhances individuals' willingness to act in accordance with their moral convictions. In this way, ethics education not only nurtures moral reasoning but also promotes the internalization of ethical values, encouraging learners to become morally responsible and socially engaged citizens.

In its broadest sense, education encompasses any act or experience that exerts a formative influence on an individual's mind, character, or physical capabilities. Etymologically, the term "education" derives from the Latin Educo, meaning to train or to lead out, reflecting its dual function of instruction and personal development. Education is fundamentally a process of learning and acquiring knowledge, skills, and values through both formal and informal means. Within this framework, the ethics of education is increasingly recognized as an essential component of the human right to education. Its purpose extends beyond the theoretical study of moral philosophy; rather, it seeks to operationalize ethical knowledge in two critical ways. First, it aims to develop individuals' cognitive capacities to identify and address ethical dimensions across diverse fields such as economics, public policy, and medicine. Second, it fosters critical thinking and reflective judgement, enabling learners to deliberate on their motivations and assess the consequences of their actions—both individually and collectively. This reflective engagement enhances moral agency and encourages individuals to act in accordance with their ethical convictions. Thus, ethics education plays a pivotal role in cultivating moral reasoning, promoting responsible behaviour, and preparing individuals to navigate complex social realities with integrity and purpose.

Education, in its general sense, refers to any act or experience that exerts a formative influence on an individual's intellect, character, or physical capabilities. Etymologically, the term "education" originates from the Latin educare, meaning to train or to lead out, reflecting its dual role in instruction and personal development. As a process of teaching and learning, education facilitates the acquisition of knowledge, skills, values, and attitudes, shaping both individual potential and societal progress. The history of education is inseparable from the history of human civilization, serving as a foundational mechanism through which individuals become socially and culturally integrated members of society. It plays a critical role in maximizing human potential and fostering the development of civilized individuals. Moreover, education functions as a conduit for the transmission of culture and heritage, enabling the intergenerational transfer of knowledge, skills, and values. Philosophical contributions from ancient Greek thinkers such as Socrates, Plato, and Aristotle laid the groundwork for many principles that underpin contemporary educational systems. Their insights continue to influence modern pedagogical thought, emphasizing the enduring relationship between education, ethical development, and the cultivation of human excellence. Across classical philosophical traditions, a shared belief persists that the fundamental purpose of education is the improvement of humankind. This principle is evident in the enduring influence of ancient Greek philosophers whose ideas continue to shape modern educational theory and practice. The Socratic Method, for instance, remains a cornerstone of contemporary pedagogy, emphasizing dialogical inquiry wherein educators pose probing questions to stimulate students' reasoning and intellectual development. Plato, the founder of idealism, envisioned education as a means to cultivate individual capacities for the betterment of society. He advocated for universal access to education, asserting that both men and women possess the right to be educated, and proposed a structured progression of educational stages tailored to human development. For Plato, education was not merely a personal endeavour but a societal imperative. In contrast, Aristotle, regarded as the father of realism, emphasized the role of education in actualizing human potential through practical engagement with the world. He maintained that education should be reserved for citizens and championed a tripartite model comprising theoretical, practical, and technical instruction. Aristotle viewed the educated individual as one who achieves fulfilment through the harmonious integration of knowledge and action. Together, these philosophical foundations continue to inform contemporary educational paradigms, highlighting the enduring relevance of classical thought in shaping the aims, methods, and ethical dimensions of education.

Education plays a pivotal role in the development of both the physical and intellectual faculties of individuals. Historically, in ancient Greece, education was regarded as a function of the state, designed to serve its broader political and social objectives. In contemporary contexts, education continues to fulfil dual roles—addressing the needs of both the state or society and the individual citizen. It is therefore recognized as a cornerstone of personal and societal advancement. Through the cultivation of knowledge, character, and civic responsibility, education contributes to the holistic development of individuals and the progress of the nation. It is instrumental in shaping complete human beings and fostering the evolution of a just and informed society. Schools, as foundational institutions within the educational framework, serve as critical environments for nurturing these values. They guide children not only in academic learning but also in becoming responsible citizens and ethically grounded individuals, thereby reinforcing the broader societal function of education. The integration of ethical education within the broader educational framework is essential for fostering morally responsible individuals and ensuring the integrity of educational institutions. Teaching ethics in schools is not merely a supplementary activity but a foundational necessity for cultivating values such as honesty, justice, and accountability. This chapter explores the role of ethics in education, addressing key questions: Why is ethics important? Why should it be taught in schools? And what forms of ethics are most appropriate for educational settings? Ethics in education can be conceptualized across four progressive stages: (1) ethics education within the family, (2) ethics education in schools, (3) ethics education at the university level, and (4) ethics education in professional and business contexts. Each stage reflects a distinct developmental phase in moral learning. In the family, children internalize ethical norms by observing the behaviour of parents and caregivers, who serve as primary role models. In schools, ethics education—often framed as character or value education—helps students distinguish between right and wrong, fostering traits such as trustworthiness, responsibility, and fairness. While ethics is frequently associated with religious instruction in many educational systems, it is imperative to move beyond doctrinal approaches and emphasize value clarification and ethical decision making. Schools play a critical role in shaping students' moral reasoning and emotional intelligence, thereby contributing to the development of ethically grounded and socially conscious individuals. At the university level, ethics education should be oriented toward professional ethics, equipping students with the moral reasoning and decision-making skills necessary for their respective fields. However, in many higher education institutions, ethics is not uniformly integrated across all disciplines; it is typically offered within select departments such as philosophy, psychology, guidance and counselling, and business studies. This limited inclusion restricts broader access to ethical training, despite its relevance across all professional domains. When offered, professional ethics courses enable students to critically evaluate moral dilemmas, make ethically sound decisions, and understand diverse moral perspectives within their fields of practice. In professional environments, such as business, individuals are introduced to occupational codes of ethics that guide conduct and promote integrity in workplace interactions.

In the context of the Turkish educational system, ethics is often conflated with religious instruction, with students typically receiving education in religious culture rather than in secular ethical reasoning. This conflation can obscure the broader philosophical and civic dimensions of ethics. While religious education may impart moral values, it does not necessarily foster the analytical skills required for ethical decision making in pluralistic and professional contexts. Therefore, educational institutions must incorporate dedicated ethics courses that emphasize value clarification, moral reasoning, and the development of ethical agency. Such an approach would better prepare students to navigate complex moral landscapes in both personal and professional spheres and contribute to the cultivation of socially responsible and ethically grounded citizens. In primary, secondary, and high school education, students are typically introduced to moral and religious instruction through courses on religious culture and morality. However, within educational theory, it is important to distinguish between the concepts of ethics and morality, which are often conflated in practice. Etymologically, *ethics* derives from the Greek word *ethos*, meaning custom or character, while *morality* originates from the Latin term *mores*, meaning custom or manner. Although both terms share a common root in the notion of custom, their philosophical meanings diverge significantly. Morality refers to a first-order system of beliefs and practices concerning how individuals ought to live a good life. Ethics, by contrast, is a second-order, reflective discipline that critically examines the validity and coherence of moral beliefs and practices.

In educational contexts, this distinction is crucial. While moral education focuses on instilling values and behavioural norms, ethics education encourages critical reflection, value clarification, and the development of moral reasoning. In many systems, including the Turkish educational framework, ethics is often subsumed under religious instruction, limiting students' exposure to secular ethical inquiry. As a result, students may not engage with ethics as a philosophical discipline until they reach university, and even then, only within select departments such as philosophy, psychology, or business studies. To foster ethically informed and socially responsible individuals, it is essential that educational systems incorporate ethics as a distinct and integral part of the curriculum, beginning at earlier stages of education.

The origins of education are deeply rooted in the history of human civilization, evolving as a fundamental mechanism for shaping individuals and societies. Education serves not only as a means of intellectual and physical development but also as a pathway toward becoming civilized and socially responsible human beings. It plays a critical role in maximizing human potential and facilitating the transmission of culture and heritage across generations. This intergenerational modern society. He highlights that humans are part of a larger ecological system and that their cultural values are inherited from tradition. By living in a social organization, humans are exposed to a complex web of inherited customs and values, which allows them to consciously and unconsciously create culture. For this reason, these core values must be taught to young students. However, Pal warns that this education should be approached neutrally and rationally, not coercively, to avoid stifling a student's creativity, wisdom, and autonomy.

Professor Avinash, in his article "Rise of Education System and Its Moral values", explores the different shades and meanings of education. He sees it as a powerful influence that shapes a child's mind, using the wisdom of previous generations to help them adapt to their surroundings. He notes that the term "education" can be used to describe many different actions, such as coaching, counselling, nurturing, or simply teaching. He analyses the evolution of education and organizes it into four distinct sections: practical education, theoretical education, value education, and the teaching class.

Dr D.R. Bhandari has contributed three articles in this volume. In two articles within this volume, Dr Bhandari expresses concern over a modern value crisis. He argues that the alienation of people from their environment, society, and themselves is eroding core human values like secularism, socialism, and democracy and normative science values. Bhandari stresses the need to cultivate "ethical-social values" and argues that because education is a powerful tool for social change, academic institutions must take on the responsibility of teaching these values. He concludes his second essay by stating that value education is a foundational guiding principle, and without it, the sustainable development of society is impossible.

Mahi Pal Singh's analysis in "Private 'Public' Schools and the Right to Education" critiques the significant flaws in India's modern educational landscape. He highlights the disconnect between the constitutional right to free and compulsory education (Article 45) and the prohibitive admission fees of private schools. Simultaneously, he notes the failure of government schools to attract students due to inadequate resources, leading to vacant positions. This duality, he argues, necessitates the abolition of such systemic distinctions.

In a subsequent article, Singh further explores the socio-economic stratification within education. He posits that private institutions cater to an elite class, while public schools are relegated to the working masses. This pronounced inequality, he suggests, is a direct consequence of a flawed educational and political system, and it threatens to create a permanent social divide between the powerful and the powerless. Singh concludes that this disparity's detrimental effects on educators and the entire teaching process demand urgent attention.

In a third article, Professor D.R. Bhandari discusses "Gandhian Thought and Modern Indian Education", he argues that the legacy of Macaulay's education system has led to a major crisis, where education is mistakenly equated with mere academic qualifications and literacy, causing it to lose its true purpose. In response, Bhandari highlights Mahatma Gandhi's reform suggestions, which aimed to develop a spiritual person dedicated to truth and non-violence. Gandhi's philosophy emphasized the importance of "basic education" and *svadeśī* (self-sufficiency).

In his article, "Philosophy and Education: The Indian Perspective", Y.V. Satyanarayana defines philosophy as a guiding principle for life and education, derived from the Greek words for "love of knowledge and wisdom". He argues that philosophy has always aimed to enhance human qualities by shaping attitudes, beliefs, and ideals, with the goal of fostering intellectual and moral development. This is evident in both ancient Indian and Greek thought.

Satyanarayana notes that for ancient Indian thinkers, the goal of education was "self-realization"—unfolding a person's inherent spiritual, physical, and psychological qualities. Therefore, the teacher's role is to remove obstacles and guide students to become "true human beings". He concludes that while modern society values science and technology, it's crucial that education also instills the ethical foundations of normative science to ensure socio-political and economic progress is guided by morality.

In her article, "Dimensions of Education: A Gandhian Perspective," Abha Singh discusses three main points: the need for basic education, the Gandhian model, and a critical analysis. She posits that modern India's education system, introduced by Macaulay, was designed to create clerks and, while it brought science and technology, it also introduced a value-neutral culture that was at odds with India's traditional value-centric education.

In contrast, Singh explains that Gandhi's educational philosophy centred on "basic education", which used handicrafts to teach village children and prepare them for modern life. The Gandhian system, which she says is comprised of physical, intellectual, social, and spiritual dimensions, merged the principles of basic education with *svadeśī*.

In her paper, "Value Education: A Critical Appraisal", Professor Sarita Kumari analyses the necessity of value education for modern individuals navigating a critical existential situation. She posits that the swift development of science, technology, and industrialization has destabilized the traditional roots of society, resulting in pervasive confusion. Consequently, she asserts a pressing need for value education that incorporates "spiritual values", with a specific focus on an individual's relationship with a supreme being.

In her essay, "Ethical Issues in Higher Education", Yamini Sahay critiques the current state of higher education, expressing concern over the extensive use of unfair practices in the examination system. She underscores the critical necessity of addressing ethical issues within the academic environment. Many institutions globally have already responded by establishing normative policies and moral codes to guide employees and students toward ethical conduct, with the broader objective of fostering ethical leaders and responsible citizens. Sahay suggests that academic institutions can facilitate this by providing numerous opportunities for students and faculty to participate in ethical initiatives and by incorporating ethics into orientation programmes.

In her essay, "Education and Swami Vivekananda: A Quest of Life", Kumkum Sinha argues that education is crucial for developing a person's full potential, not just for achieving high exam scores. She believes that education should cultivate a virtuous vision that helps individuals distinguish between right and wrong. Sinha connects this to the current moral crisis, where scientific development has dehumanized people and undermined social values. She advocates for a return to ancient Indian value education to awaken humanity's "pristine wisdom". Drawing on Vivekananda's philosophy, she states that education is a tool for social improvement, achieved by teaching virtues from the Vedas, Upaniṣads, and other sacred texts.

In a separate article, "Education and Globalization: A Philosophical Study", Sinha defines globalization as the process of unifying the world into a single society. However, she notes that in the late twentieth century, globalization coincided with a period of social and moral chaos, marked by exploitation, corruption, and environmental degradation. In this context, she concludes that value education is more necessary than ever.

Rajjan Kumar and Sunita Kumari, in "Education, Ethics and Value", assert that education is the key to human development, as it transmits knowledge and moral values. They reference Swami Vivekananda to emphasize that the goal of education isn't just to provide information, but to build a person's character and their life. For them, education is a constant process of both gaining and passing on knowledge that is rooted in values.

transfer of knowledge, skills, and values has long been recognized as a central human endeavour. In ancient Greece, philosophers such as Socrates, Plato, and Aristotle made enduring contributions to educational thought, many of which continue to influence contemporary pedagogical practices. Central to this legacy is the Socratic Method, which remains a vital instructional strategy in modern education. Through guided questioning, educators encourage students to engage in reflective reasoning and critical inquiry, thereby enhancing their intellectual capacities. Collectively, these classical perspectives underscore a shared belief that the ultimate purpose of education is the moral and intellectual advancement of humankind. Contemporary educational theories are deeply rooted in the philosophical foundations laid by classical thinkers such as Plato and Aristotle. Plato, the founder of idealism and the Academy—widely regarded as the first university—envisioned education as a means to cultivate individual capacities for the betterment of society. He advocated for universal access to education, asserting that both men and women possess the right to be educated, and proposed a structured progression of educational stages aligned with human development. For Plato, education was not only a personal right but a societal necessity. In contrast, Aristotle, the progenitor of realism, emphasized the role of education in actualizing human potential through engagement with the empirical world. He believed that education should be reserved for citizens and championed a tripartite model encompassing theoretical, practical, and technical instruction. Aristotle viewed the educated individual as one who achieves fulfilment through the harmonious integration of knowledge and action.

In ancient Greece, education was conceived as a function of the state, designed to serve its broader civic and political objectives. This view persists in modern educational systems, where education continues to address both societal needs and individual development. It contributes to character formation, intellectual growth, and the advancement of the state. Schools, as foundational institutions, play a critical role in this process by shaping students into responsible citizens and ethically grounded individuals. The enduring relevance of classical pedagogical methods, such as the Socratic Method—which promotes intellectual inquiry through guided questioning—underscores the importance of ethical education in cultivating reflective and morally responsible learners. Therefore, embedding ethics within school curricula is essential for fostering holistic development and preparing individuals to contribute meaningfully to society. The role of ethics in education is both foundational and multifaceted, raising critical questions about its importance, its place within curricula, and the nature of ethical instruction appropriate for different educational stages. Ethics education can be conceptualized across four progressive domains:

(1) ethics education within the family,
(2) ethics education in schools,
(3) ethics education at the university level, and
(4) ethics education in professional and business contexts.

Each stage reflects a distinct phase in the moral and cognitive development of individuals. In the family setting, ethical learning begins through observation and imitation, as children internalize social norms and values by witnessing the behaviours of parents and caregivers, who serve as primary role models. This early exposure to ethical conduct lays the groundwork for moral reasoning. In schools, ethics education—often framed as character or value education—helps students distinguish between right and wrong, fostering traits such as trustworthiness, responsibility, and justice. However, in many educational systems, ethics is frequently conflated with religious instruction, resulting in the substitution of ethics courses with religious culture classes. While religious education may impart moral values, it does not necessarily cultivate the analytical and reflective skills required for ethical decision making. Therefore, it is essential that students engage in value clarification and learn to navigate ethical dilemmas through reasoned judgement.

At the university level, ethics education should evolve into professional ethics, tailored to the specific moral challenges of various disciplines. Despite its relevance, ethics is not universally offered across all departments; it is typically confined to fields such as philosophy, psychology, counselling, and business. This limited access restricts students' ability to critically engage with ethical issues pertinent to their future professions. In professional contexts, such as business, ethics education introduces individuals to occupational codes of conduct, guiding behaviour and promoting integrity in workplace settings.

To ensure the development of ethically grounded individuals capable of contributing responsibly to society, ethics must be integrated systematically across all levels of education—not merely as a moral supplement, but as a core component of intellectual and civic formation. Ethics education plays a critical role in shaping students' moral reasoning and professional integrity, particularly at the university level, where it should be aligned with disciplinary and occupational contexts. Professional ethics courses help students discern ethical principles relevant to their fields, enabling them to make informed decisions and evaluate diverse moral perspectives. In business education, for example, students are introduced to codes of conduct that guide behaviour in professional settings, reinforcing accountability and ethical standards.

However, the integration of ethics education across educational systems remains uneven. In the Turkish context, ethics is often conflated with religious instruction, resulting in the predominance of religious culture courses throughout primary, secondary, and high school education. This conflation limits students' exposure to secular ethical reasoning and critical moral inquiry. Ethics as a distinct academic discipline is typically introduced only at the university level, and even then, it is confined to select departments such as philosophy, psychology, guidance, and counselling, and business studies. Consequently, many students complete their formal education without engaging in structured ethical reflection or decision-making frameworks.

This gap underscores the need for a more inclusive and systematic approach to ethics education across all levels of schooling. Ethical instruction should not be restricted to religious or professional contexts but should encompass value clarification, moral reasoning, and the development of ethical agency. In light of this, it is timely and relevant to present a synthesis of scholarly contributions from Indian academics, whose work offers valuable insights into the integration of ethics within diverse educational frameworks.

Professor R. C. Sinha's essay "Value Education" presents Sri Aurobindo's educational philosophy. Aurobindo envisioned a national education system centred on understanding the human mind's inherent potential for learning. He believed education serves two key functions:

*Informative:* This function addresses physical needs and comfort.

*Transformative:* This function goes deeper, fostering social reform by instilling values, a sense of duty, and responsibility in individuals. The goal is to produce high-quality citizens who contribute to both their own lives and society as a whole.

Jagat Pal's article "Some Philosophical Reflections on the Moral Value Education" outlines a dual approach to moral education. First, it should impart moral knowledge, teaching students the difference between right and good. Second, it should cultivate moral character, instilling habits that lead to virtuous behaviour and help build a civil society. Pal believes this is essential to combat the erosion of values in

D.C. Srivastava, in his scholarly article "Buddhist Ethics and Education", draws a key distinction between Western and Buddhist educational goals. While Western education often prioritizes physical comfort, Buddhist education is designed to help a student fully unlock their inherent potential. This system is structured around three core components: Ethics (*śīla*), Contemplation (*samādhi*), and Wisdom (*pañña*). He explains that ethical training is essential for mental development, which then provides the foundation for gaining wisdom.

In his three articles within this anthology, Sohan Raj Tater consistently emphasizes the critical need for moral and value-centric ethics. He posits that the modern focus on informative knowledge, despite its capacity to generate wealth and sensory enjoyment, ultimately contributes to profound frustration. Consequently, he advocates for a shift toward moral teachings and value-based education, which he identifies as a prerequisite for "sustainable development". Tater defines peace and value education as the process of internalizing values and fostering attitudes that promote respect for human dignity and the environment.

Archana Srivastava's article, "On Creating the Ecologically Responsible Culture", posits that true moral change cannot happen without an internal transformation of our intellect, loyalties, affections, and core beliefs. She suggests that for education to be effective, "environmental literacy" must go beyond just scientific facts and instead focus on reshaping personal loyalties and convictions.

In her scholarly chapter "Evaluation in Teacher Education is a Tool for Quality Sustainability", Dr Shashirekha S.M. posits that because teachers are the cornerstone of any educational programme, their evaluation is paramount for sustaining quality. She explains that evaluating a teacher's proficiency and competence is a necessary process to determine their professional growth and adaptability to contemporary educational needs.

**Shiva Nath Prasad**
**Avinash Kumar Srivastava**

# 1

# Value Education

*R.C. Sinha*

An important feature of educational development in India during past several decades has been the sustained effort to evolve a national system of education. It was Sri Aurobindo, who first of all in the year 1910, visualized "A National System of Education". Its main emphasis was on the nature and power of the human mind, the nature of simultaneous and successive teaching and the training of mental and logical faculty. Gandhiji's *buniyādī tālīm* (basic education) as envisaged in the Wardha scheme was another powerful indigenous model rooted firmly in the Indian soil. The curriculum developed under this scheme aimed at the total development of the child reflecting the Gandhian philosophy of education, Indian philosophy of education aims at development of body, mind, and spirit.

> "Human beings have a natural potential for learning the potentiality and desire for learning, for discovery, for enlargement of conditions. It is a tendency which can be trusted and the wide approach to education builds upon and around the student's natural desire to learn."[1]

## The Meaning of Education

I take education as the cultivation of values. Generally, the scope of education can be divided along *two types*, namely, "informative" and "transformative". Informative education fulfils our needs, our comforts and own livelihood on the physical plane. The technicians, doctors, scientists, administrators, lawyers, professionals are the products of this informative education. There is need to put concerted effort to produce creative people who can be both effective and efficient. The education which brings a social transformation in life and human societies can be termed as transformative education, which is "value based". The aim of education is to "produce quality of individual". We have to give attention towards the "imparting life values" in the individual and imbibe the "sense of duty and responsibility in each and every individual". Personality development programme among students, or teachers has been accepted as necessary training to learn confidence, pleasant approach, intense effort, etc., to succeed in life. Nobody disputes the importance of these qualities. But the value education has another important facets of human values, i.e., social values and national values. An Indian delegate met Sir John F. Kennedy, the then President of America and asked about some reasons of excellent infrastructure and meaningful education system in America. He replied to the delegates, "Every teacher in America looks at every student of America as a future"—President of America. So, we should also make our teacher understand their responsibility and vision and make our students to take care of individual, family, social, and national duties and responsibilities through necessary will and necessary efficiency.

We all know the great sufferings of Japan in building the nation. Two reasons were put forth for Japan's growth. The attempt to educate the society in general and the new generations in particular.

(a) First, team spirit—"The necessity for collective responsibility was made essential". We have to work together to rebuild and develop our Japan and while doing so, we have to give up our individual ego, prestige, selfishness, etc. "This was the written pledge of the ordinary Japanese."

(b) The second aspect was more important. "They (Japanese) have seen trained to withstand the temporary setbacks for themselves for the sake of permanent gains to their country. This aspect was also conveyed very strongly and the necessary collective mentality was built. These two aspects which made the revival and strong growth of Japan are very much necessary for our country's revival of growth too, after more than 1,000 years of depression under foreign rule.

## Action Plan for Value Education

Thus, through teaching and teacher training, there is an urgent need to give "vision", "direction", and "inspiration" to teachers and new generations. Having this in mind, we can move forward in giving value-based education by taking into consideration the following facts while preparing the curricula, the teaching materials and subjects.

> "By accepting a position as a teacher, a person has not only a right but an 'obligation' to modify student behaviour. Children enter the schools without the necessary social and academic skills to function independently and productively in adult society.... Teachers who do not bring about suitable changes in student behaviour are failing to live up to the responsibility of the profession."[2]

### (a) ***Career Meant for National Reconstruction and Social Service***

The aim of education should not be only for livelihood or career building and through them earning money to lead a comfortable life with one's family only. Even for own profession or career there is a purpose. That is, through my profession I will strive in reconstructing this country of mine, in elevating the prestige of the country and in helping my fellow countrymen. Never should I exploit my people through my profession.

### (b) ***National Identity***

Knowledge about our country's core essence and emphasis on national identity. Even after 75 years of Independence, our people have not understood the real meaning of *svarājya* or *svatantratā* or freedom. Freedom has been equalled with political freedom only. Freedom or Independence also means realizing and safeguarding this country's soul. Teaching curricula should be prepared to make our cultural and national distinctiveness alive. Students and teachers should safeguard national identity. The task of the teacher is to prepare students to become ideal citizen. According to the former education minister Shri Kalu Lal Srimali "The task of educationist is to reconstruct and redefine values, so that, they may interpret our changing life and thought". Education is only explicit formulation of the problem of formulation of right mental and moral altitude in respect of the difficulties of post-modern social life. Education does not commence with alphabet rather it, "begins with mother's look with father's nod of approbation". Abraham Lincoln the then President of America once said, "a child learns the best lessons of citizenship between kisses of mothers and care of fathers". Education is all-round development of whole personality of man.

Real education has to draw out the best from the boys and girls to be educated. This can never be done by packing all efforts and unwanted information into the heads of the students. It becomes a dead weight crushing all originality in them and turning them into mere automata. It stifles creativity.[3]

The task of building an enlightened, strong and prosperous nation rests on the shoulders of teachers. Education reflects its main ethos, aspiration, and concerns.

The Education Policy of 2020, which is known as New Education Policy envisages a radical transformation of the education system to release it more closely to the lives of the people, provide expanded educational opportunities, initiate a sustained intensive effort to raise the quality of education at all stages, emphasize the development of science and technology and cultivate moral and social values.

## NOTES

1. Columbus Carl Rogers (1969). *Freedom to Learn*, Charles E. Merrill Publishing Company, U.S.A., pp. 157-58.
2. Axelrod, Said (1997). *Behaviour Modification for Classroom Teachers,* New York: McGraw Hill, p. 158.
3. Mahatma Gandhi, *Harijan*, 1 December 1933.

# 2

# Some Philosophical Reflections on the Moral Value Education

*Jagat Pal*

The objective for introducing the programme of moral value education at school level is said of twofold:

(i) to impart information to students about what is good and right, so that, they can plan and take the right course of action in their pursuit of the good;

(ii) to improve the character of students by inculcating habits in them to act virtuously as a good person acts and produce a civil society.

But then the question arises: can we really make students virtuous by imparting information about what are good and right and inculcating habits in them to act virtuously by the programme of moral value education? What cultural moral values should be taught to students in multicultural societies like India? If it is not possible for us to make students virtuous by inculcating habits in them to act virtuously as a good person acts by the programme of moral value education, is it not self-defeating? And if it is possible to make students virtuous by inculcating habits in them to act virtuously as a good person acts by the programme of moral value education, does it not go against the very basic moral postulate of human freedom which is considered a necessary condition to be virtuous? In other words, if it is true that the idea of moral virtue logically rests on the idea of individual's freedom and the idea of individual's freedom is incompatible with idea of indoctrination of virtues, because it involves in it the idea of force, or imposition from the outside, does it not go against the basic moral postulate of individual's freedom on which it logically rests? If so, does it not prevent moral educators and schools from indoctrinating in, or imposing their own values, or the values of their own traditions on students? If not, does it not allow students to sort out and practice a code of conduct of their own? If it does, does it not go against the very premise of value driven approach to character education? A critical reflection on it clearly shows that it does go against the very premise of value driven approach to character education because the objective of value driven approach to character education is said to make students virtuous by creating habits in them to act virtuously as a good person acts which is not possible without moral educators and schools to exercise certain measures of control over students because any activity in order to qualify as a form of character education necessarily presupposes it. Even if we admit for the sake of argument that the value driven approach to character education does not necessarily presuppose it, the question still remains: does the value driven approach to character education necessarily command students' behaviour and make their life a better life? Does imparting of moral value education really guide students to make plan and take the right course of action in the pursuits of theirs individual and social goodness in actual circumstances? It is generally said, character education is accomplished largely by means of the students' own purely autonomous insight and not by inculcating habits in them to act virtuously, according to what the educators and schools think and feel that they ought to act to be virtuous within a society. If so, does it not imply that students should be given full autonomy to frame their own views on what they think is virtuous and what is not in building of their character? If it does, does it not defeat the very objective of value driven approach to character education? If it is said that the notion of virtue logically rests on the notion of freedom, does it not imply that virtues arise purely from individual's autonomous insight? It is generally said that the notion of virtue involves in it the notion of rationality because to be virtuous is to be reasonable and to be reasonable is to rationalize, construct and adhere to a code of one's own conduct and not to what tradition prescribes or moral educators and schools think and feel that students ought to act to be virtuous. If so, does it not imply that virtues are not fixed absolute dispositions or traits of character? Both the lines of thought pose a number of philosophical issues. This chapter intends to discuss and examine some of these issues. And through the analysis an attempt also will be made to show that the programme of moral value education is not a meaningless programme. It is quite a meaningful programme both individually as well as socially. It is required by all societies, but not at the cost of individual's creativity, wisdom, autonomy and rationality. Fundamental moral values not only can be taught effectively to students, but also should be taught and indoctrinated in them at their initial stage of life, if not at the higher level, within a society regardless of whether or not it is a multicultural society, but by honouring student's creativity, wisdom, autonomy and rationality. It is for these reasons the programme of moral value driven approach to character education is, I say, not only a desirable programme, but also is necessarily required by the societies in the present age because of continuing degeneration of virtues among individuals and societies. Students' intellectual views on virtues may be different cultural settings, conceptual frameworks and knowledge. But this does not necessitate that the programme of moral value education should be discarded. We should honour this programme. Students' intellectual views on virtues do not create any difficulty in carrying out the pursuit of value driven approach to character in a society. It rather enables students to build-up their character. In fact, it is a moral responsibility of every person, parent, school, government, and society to build-up and improve the character of individuals by controlling their behaviour according to one's own moral wisdom and make them to act as a good person acts so that we can have a civil society but not at all at the cost of individual's intellectual creativity, wisdom, autonomy, and rationality. Any society to be good always requires good citizens; and to produce good citizens indoctrination of certain fundamental moral values in its citizens are essentially required. So, mere imparting of information to students about what a morally good and right is not good enough to make them a virtuous person and a good citizens. Practice also is equally and essentially required on their parts.

It is a well-known biological fact that all organic beings live as integral parts of larger ecological system. Human beings are no exception to it. But one thing unique about human beings is that they are creatures of culture to a greater extent than any other organic being. They grow into social organizations that have complex sets of shared customs and values which enable them to communicate with one another within the society. Human beings inherit values from their own cultural traditions to which they belong, consciously or unconsciously. In inheriting of cultural values they also observe where its drawbacks as well as its benefits are. But to say all this, however, does not mean that human beings are essentially culture-structured, they cannot transcend then own cultural settings. There is no doubt in it that human character is by and large formed by its cultural settings. But at the same time it is also equally true that it is human beings who set new cultural values from time-to-time to cater to the needs of the society either by discarding or by improving their own traditional cultural values. This is possible simply because human thinking is not essentially culture-structured, human mind has a capacity to transcend its all cultural boundaries whatsoever. Historical cultural revolutions and progress confer it. If at all it were not so, there would have no Cultural Revolution in the history of mankind, it would have not been possible for us to view ourselves and our actions from the point of view of others or examine, evaluate and pass value judgements on the other's culture as well as one's own. But this is not true. As a matter of reality, we all do examine, evaluate and pass value judgements not only on our culture, but also on the other's culture which itself clearly shows that human thinking is not essentially culture structured. It is rather essentially culture-free, it has a capacity to go beyond all its cultural boundaries. Moreover, the value driven approach to character education does not contradict human thinking is not essentially culture-structured. The value driven approach to character education rather assumes human thinking is not culture-structured because it recognizes the individual's intellectual creativity, wisdom, knowledge, autonomy, and rationality. If any pursuit of value driven approach to character education does not recognize human thinking is not essentially culture-structured, it is not a genuine value driven approach to character education at all in my considered opinion. Since school children do not know what is morally good and right, therefore, they always require from their respective society some kind of information about what is morally good and right to shape their character. Besides, they also require indoctrination of certain fundamental moral virtues in them at their initial stage of life in building up their character. But all this should be done in a conscious, rational, careful, neutral, and objective manner without imposing one's own views on them or taking the side of any specific cultural values or religious tradition. The objective of moral educators and schools should be to present fundamental moral virtues to students and also to indoctrinate in them through the enactment of certain virtues governing rules, but not at the cost of theirs intellectual growth, creativity, wisdom, autonomy, and rationality, because these things are also equally required by students in building up their virtuous character within a society.

Virtues are of different kinds. Some virtues are primarily private but most are not either in origin or influence. Some virtues are moral; some virtues are religious or intellectual. But all virtues, nonetheless, are dispositions cultivated by the individuals under certain specific social environment. The character of an individual depends upon the nature and cultivation of virtues when we judge the character of any individual, we always judge it by referring to his/her conduct. Character and conduct are conceptually connected. Conduct constitutes criterion by which we assess the character of person. Our intellectual views and interpretations on what constitutes virtues and vices may be different. As a matter of reality, in fact, they do differ but our different views and interpretations on them do not create any difficulty. Prudence, humility, modesty, diligence, integrity, sincerity, punctuality, obedience, dutifulness, law abidingness, accountability, courage, wisdom, justice, temperance, honesty, generosity, truthfulness, compassion (*karuṇā*), tolerance, self-dignity, self-respect, discipline, hospitality, self-sacrifice, benevolence, confidence, idlelessness, self-esteem, friendliness (*metta*), joy (*mudita*), equanimity (*upekṣā*), non-violence (*ahiṁsā*), non-stealing, celibacy, gratitude and commitment, etc. are generally called moral virtues and all these moral virtues are not of the same kind. Some moral virtues among them are primarily private in origin and influence (for example, diligence and self-dignity), but most of them are not (for example, generosity and self-sacrifice). Generosity is not a private virtue. It is a public virtue. Its applicability is not restricted to by the specificities of any particular culture, race or religion. It is a cross-cultural, cross-racial and cross-religious moral virtue. From this point of view, we can very well say that generosity is a universal moral value. It is praised and prescribed in all cultures, races, and religions. People praised and prescribed it in all cultures, races, and religions simply because it preserves, protects and nourishes human goodness of all in all times regardless of their specific culture, religion, and race. But to say all this, however, does not mean to say that it is intrinsic to human nature. It only means that it is a universal moral virtue. Its applicability and validity are not restricted to by the specificities of any particular culture, religion or race. And when we say it, it does not mean that it is intrinsic to human nature. Had it been so, human beings would have had it genetically by nature; they would have inherited it from their forefathers without its cultivation; they would have simply owned it. But this is not true because we all acquire it through our continuous conscious efforts. If we admit for the sake of argument that human beings possess it intrinsically, then it makes no sense for us to talk about making students virtuous by inculcating habits in them to act virtuously as a good person acts which is considered to be one of the objectives of the value driven approach to character education, because what it intends to achieve, that students will already have it by nature. But this is not true because none of us is virtuous or vicious by our nature. We cannot say is that we are virtuous intrinsically, but vicious extrinsically, because it is the same moral principle, when it is obeyed makes one virtuous and vicious, when it is disobeyed. We acquire virtuous and vicious qualities by doing virtuous and vicious deeds after taking the birth. Virtuous and vicious qualities are not inborn biological human qualities. They are not factual qualities either. Virtues and vices are values and disvalues respectively which we human beings have constructed interest and the interest of our species. They are conceptually connected with our nations of value and disvalues which we entertain about certain kinds of things within our society and these things vary, because of our different conception of moral world view. But to say this does not mean that each moral world view is equally rational or irrational which it is not. It only implies that there are different moral rationalities. Even if we admit for the sake of argument that each moral world view is equally rational or irrational, we can do it only when we logically assume is that they share a common ground because the former always presupposes the later.

Like voters, some vices are primarily private, but most are not either in origin or influence. Cruelty, killing, stealing, adultery, false speech, jealousy (*īrṣyā*), maddening drinks, exploitation, hatred and enmity, etc., are clear examples of public moral vices. These moral vices cause havoc to our social life when we practise them within a society. Attachment (*āsakti*), anger (*krodha*), greed (*lobha*), craving (*tṛṣṇā*), pride (*mada*), delusions (*māyā*), cowardice, etc., are clear examples of private vices. These moral vices cause havoc mostly to our private life. But no virtues or vices are purely private or public, because all virtues and vices do have some causal impact directly or indirectly not only on our private life, but also on our public life. It is because of this reason we all bother about virtues and vices in our inter-personal life. We become virtuous by doing virtuous deeds and vicious by doing vicious deeds in certain manner but within a society. There is nothing in our human nature that makes us either virtuous or vicious. In other words, virtues and vices are all human cultivated qualities within the society. They are not constitutive ingredients of our being. They also are not physical realities of the external world either. They are mere constructions of our human mind, which we human beings have constructed to safeguard our own private and public interests and the interest of our own species. It is because of these reasons human beings have been praising virtues and condemning vices throughout in the history of human civilization. But to say all this does not mean to say that moral virtues and vices are not intrinsic to human nature.

Why do we all have different intellectual views and interpretations on what constitute virtues and vices? We do have different intellectual views and interpretations on what constitutes virtues and vices simply because there are no absolute norms of virtues and vices which could be said to be eternal, permanent, and valid under all circumstances. What we consider virtuous and vicious in our society may or may not be considered virtuous and vicious by another people in their own respective societies. In different cultures different people have identified different virtues and vices. But no matter what views and interpretations we may hold on them, we always cultivate and possess them within a society and it is our virtues, not our views and interpretations on them that enable us to shape and lead a healthier private and public life. The cultivation of a particular virtue always requires a particular social environment. We cannot cultivate all virtues under any social environment. In other words, if we do not have a particular social environment which the practice of a particular virtue requires, we cannot simply practice it even if we wish. For example, we cannot cultivate generosity virtue in a world where everyone had everything they wanted or chastity virtue in a world which is wholly asexual. All virtues are dispositions or habits to act in certain manner within a society, but under a certain particular social environment and not in any social environment. But none of us becomes virtuous just by doing single act of virtue because virtue is a habit or disposition to act in certain continuously under all possible circumstances and times. If there exists a conflict between two or more than two moral values within a particular social environment, we should always go by that moral value, which has relatively more weightage in the context. When we do it, we not only thereby improve and build-up our virtuous character, but also set a role model for other persons within a society.

Moral virtues are not devoid of individual and social contents. They involve in them benefits and goodness of all regardless of their culture, caste, creed, sex, etc. That is the reason why we all want to keep them than to discard or abandon. To be a virtuous person in complete sense means to become a morally perfect being. Here we might ask: how is it possible? Can we really create virtue in individuals and improve their character by inculcating habits in them to act virtuously, and hence produce a civil society? When we go through the writings of different moral philosophers, we find two opposite views on it. Those who assume the premise that human freedom is a necessary condition to be virtuous say that we cannot create virtues in individual and improve their character by inculcating habits in them to act virtuously because it involves force from the outside which goes against the very dictum of moral freedom which it assumes. The cultivation of virtues, in their view, always involves in it the individual's autonomy and individual's autonomy gets hampered the movement when we try impose certain sets of values on them from the outside by force. But those who do not assume the premise that human freedom is a necessary condition to be virtuous say that we can definitely make people virtuous by inculcating habits in them to act virtuously through the enactment of laws. But, nonetheless, they all agree on this point that virtues are not essential qualities of human beings. They are acquired human qualities which human beings acquire through their continuous conscious efforts within the society. The only difference that lies between them is that the former treats the element of human freedom as an essential component of the notion of virtue while the latter does not.

Let us examine the first view. According to this view, what is required to be virtuous is not just mere performance of the acts of virtues. It also requires the exercise of the individual's autonomy in deciding and performing the acts of virtues. Since the notion of virtue, in their view, essentially involves in it the notion of human freedom, therefore, they say that we cannot make people virtuous just by indoctrinating in them certain traditional cultural and social moral values through education and political means. The rules of educational system require students to comply with pre-established cultural norms and values. But virtuous people do not simply follow the prescribed norms and values of their tradition. They follow what they think is virtuous in their own practical wisdom; and what they think is virtuous in their own practical wisdom may or may not coincide with the norms and values of their own cultural tradition or the character of *mahājana*s. Virtues do not result from nor are validated by the character of a person. The virtuous character of a person is derived from the conduct of his virtuous deeds and the notion of virtue always comes logically prior to the performance of virtuous conduct. When we call a person virtuous, we call because he does virtuous deeds. We do not call a deed virtuous because it is done by a virtuous person. When we call a deed is virtuous, we call only when it conforms the conditions of virtues. The notion of moral virtuous deed is conceptually connected with the notion of moral virtue and the notion of moral virtue is conceptually connected with the notions of moral values of goodness and rightness, and not with the notion of a character of person. A virtuous person is a person of practical wisdom (*prajñā*) and knowledge (*jñāna*). He not only acts virtuously, but also knows why does he act virtuously? The notion of practical wisdom is conceptually connected with the notion of virtue and practical wisdom may differ from person to person and context to context. From this point of view, we can very well say that virtue-based ethics is not only an ethics of conduct, but also is an ethics of practical wisdom and knowledge. If this view of mine is correct, then from this it is quite evident that we can neither create nor can we indoctrinate virtues in others by force. If we make an attempt to create virtues in others against their autonomy and do not allow them to choose freely what they think is virtuous and what is not in building up their character, we cannot hold them morally responsible on the account of their character and deeds because the notion of moral responsibility always logically presupposes the notion of individual's freedom. Legal laws are not good means for making people virtuous because we cannot legislate virtues. If we try to legislate virtues, we are bound to fail because it not only goes against the very spirit of the notion of virtue, but also hinders development and goodness of the individuals and the society. Take, for example, generosity virtue. Generosity is a public virtue. We cannot cultivate it outside the society because its practice always requires respect and sympathy for others, and respect and sympathy for others we can neither legislate nor can we generate. The law cannot compel or make people to respect and have others. Respect and sympathy are human cultivated feelings. They spring from our heart. He who does not have any concern for the other's happiness, welfare and goodness or does not acknowledge human worth and dignity as fundamental human moral values cannot cultivate the feelings of respect and sympathy for others which are always required by the practice of generosity virtue within a society. The effort to create virtues by legislation destroys the very nature of thing it is intended to bring about. Virtues are, no doubt, habits or dispositions to act in certain way under certain social environments. They are traits of character. But to say this does not mean that a virtuous character is not open to critical examinations and reassessment. The characters of *mahājana*s are open to critical examinations and reassessment, and these things are possible only when we logically assume the premise that human freedom, creativity, practical wisdom, and rationality are conceptually linked with the formation of a virtuous character. To exercise one's autonomy and intelligence does not necessarily mean discarding or over throwing of our traditional cultural and social moral values and norms set by *mahājana*s. It only means that a virtuous person is a rational, enlightened, autonomous and open-minded person; he is not a mere puppet of his traditional, cultural and social moral values and norms; he does not follow the conduct of *mahājana*s simply on this ground because it is the conduct of *mahājana*s; he does what he thinks any rational and conscientious virtuous persons would think and do under all possible social environments. In other words, a virtuous person critically reflects as a rational and responsible person on what he intends to do before choosing and doing. He is a person of self-discipline. He does not do actions just by his mere habit. That is the reason why we hold him morally responsible on the account of whatever he does good or bad. A virtuous person when he finds in his critical examinations that his traditional cultural and social moral values and norms are rational and worth practising, he cultivates and prescribes them; or else he discards them and evolves new values and norms which he thinks in his practical wisdom and knowledge are virtuous in character. It is quite evident from these things that a virtuous person is not a rigid person. He is a dynamic and open-minded person. He takes into account the prevailing social environments, conditions, and needs of the society. And in doing so it is perfectly quite possible that he may or may not go wrong. But, he never assumes his traditional, cultural, and social moral values and norms as static, absolute, eternal, permanent, and valid under all social conditions and environments for everyone. He takes them only as a mere guidelines. For him moral values and norms always admit exceptions under certain social conditions and circumstances. Moral values and norms are not universally valid like the natural laws regardless of the individuals' abilities and their social environments and conditions. They hold well only in the cases of similar persons in similar conditions and circumstances. Moral values and norms are not universally valid like the natural laws regardless of the individuals' abilities and their social environments and conditions. They hold well only in the cases of similar persons in similar conditions and circumstances. A virtuous person adheres to a code of one's own. But to say this does not mean that a virtuous person is an arbitrary person. A virtuous person is not an arbitrary person. He is a conscientious, enlightened, rational, responsible and self-disciplined person. He does not act on the subjective maxims. He acts on the objective maxims which he thinks any rational person would approve and act upon it in any given appropriate social conditions and environments. A virtuous person is, thus, a person of self-dignity. Self-disciplined and self-responsibility. He does not act on the whimsical grounds nor does he prescribe any irrational principle to others which he thinks goes against the interest of society at large. But, it is perfectly quite possible what he thinks may or may not be the case because there exists no logical connection between the two.

There is no doubt in it that freedom is an essential component to be virtuous. But it does not mean that virtues can neither be taught to students nor can they be indoctrinated in them by education. Virtues can definitely be taught to students and also can be indoctrinated in them by education at school level simply because students do not know what is morally good and right at this age which is required by them to shape their character. It is for this reason students always require certain information about what is morally good and right and also indoctrination of certain fundamental moral values in them which are considered to be universal (*sāmānya dharma*) in nature to build-up their moral character in their initial stage of life. When we impart some information about what is morally good and right to students and also indoctrinate certain fundamental universal moral values in them in a neutral and rational manner, it does not hamper in any way theirs individual autonomy, creativity and rationality. It hampers only when we do not acknowledge and honour theirs autonomy, practical wisdom and creativity and impose our own religious and cultural views on them forcefully by rules and laws. Once students develop their own rational faculty and also know what is morally right and wrong, they themselves can scrutinize values indoctrinated in them and form their own independent opinion on them. This is how virtues are cultivated and developed by the individuals including *mahājana*s when we grow in age within a society. It is true that freedom is a necessary condition to be virtuous, but freedom alone does not make any person virtuous. Besides freedom, practical wisdom, and rationality are also equally and essentially required. Freedom without solf-discipline, practical wisdom and rationality is futile. It is neither desirable nor is conducive to the formation, development and increase of a virtuous character because these elements are embedded in our conception of a virtuous character.

Let us examine the second view. According to this view, we can make people virtuous just by creating habits in them to act virtuously as a good person acts by the means of education and political systems because what is required, in their view, to be virtuous is just a mere performance of the acts of virtues and the acts of virtues can be performed freely or unfreely. The individual's autonomy does not come into its picture at all. In other words, we become virtuous just by performing the acts of virtues whenever and wherever they are required to be done within a social environment, no matter whether we do them freely or under the compulsion. For example, we become just by doing just action and courageous by doing courageous action no matter whether we do them freely or unfreely. Our modes or manners behind in doing of virtuous deeds are irrelevant. Freedom is not at all a necessary condition to be virtuous. Since, in their view, freedom is not an essential component to be virtuous, we can very well create virtues in students the way we like by the means of education and political systems. For them educational rules and political laws are good and effective means not only to restrain our vices, but also to improve our character by increasing virtues in us. It is for these reasons, they say, moral educators and schools frame rules and also try to make students virtuous by inculcating habits in them to act virtuously as a good person acts and in doing so if some amount of force has been used, it is morally justified. If our educational rules and legal laws do not succeed in achieving this intended goal, their legislation is failure. According to this account, virtues, thus, can be created in individuals by the means of education and political systems. Authoritative commands and penalties attached to rules and laws make students a better person and a better citizen. If this view is true, then from this it is quite evident that the society can definitely improve the character of students just by indoctrinating in them certain virtues which the society in its practical wisdom thinks are desirable through the enactment of rules and laws. Even if these things go against the students' autonomy, rationally, practical wisdom, desire, and feeling. If there is no inclination in students to be virtuous, it can be induced in them through the enactment of rules and flaws made by schools, government and society from time-to-time because virtues for them are nothing, but habits of doing certain actions in certain manner and these habits can be created through the enactment of rules and flaws.

There is no doubt in it that virtues can be taught to students and also can be indoctrinated in them by the means of education and political systems simply because they lack wisdom and knowledge; they do not live by a code of virtuous conduct they have constructed themselves nor even by one they have thought about critically to any large extent. What to say of students, even most of us live by our own traditional cultural and social moral values and norms simply on this ground because these values and norms are accepted and practised by others who have accepted them for some good reasons and there is nothing wrong in doing so also unless we have a better reason not to act upon them because whether an action is virtuous or not depends on the reason for which it is done. But while indoctrinating of our own traditional cultural and social moral values in students we will have to be very careful, rational, and critical because these values are also found embedded in our respective religious traditions. We will have to distinguish moral virtues from religious ones. Moral virtues are different from religious virtues. Moral virtues are secular while religious virtues are not. To say this does not mean that moral virtues are incompatible with religious virtues. Moral virtues may or may not be incompatible with religious virtues. So, also is the case vice versa. In fact, we cannot conceive religions virtues without morality because morality peeped into them, but we can conceive moral virtues without religion because religious beliefs do sat peep into our conception of secular morality. Whether we like or not, it is a concrete reality that we are all divided into different religious sects and each religious sect has its own different ideologies forms of faith and worship which are considered by its followers as holy. These differences are quite often used by the politicians as a weapon to create violent conflicts among different groups of people within a society. It is for this reason while preventing traditional moral values to students and indoctrinating in them in multicultural societies like India we will have to be very careful, rational, neutral, and objective; we should not take the side of any particular religion or culture prevailing within the society. But whatsoever moral values we may choose in our own moral wisdom to present students and indoctrinate in them, we should never do it at the cost of students' creativity, practical wisdom, rationality and autonomy because these elements also do constitute as ingredients of our conception of a virtuous character. The character education does not amount to simply a lesson or course on moral values. It should also enable students to develop good dispositions and flourish intellectually so that they can form their own independent opinions on virtues and act accordingly in the actual situations they come across. If we do not do so, many people would not like to send their children to school because it generates fear in them that their children might be indoctrinated with specific religious beliefs which they may not like to be indoctrinated. But to say this does not mean that one should transcend all traditional cultural and social moral values and norms to virtuous. It only means that moral virtues should be taught to students and indoctrinated in them in a secular manner. To be secular is to be rational. If student's intellectual views on virtues are rational, we should always honour and welcome them openly without any ego no matter whether or not these views come from a child or from an adult person. We should always give information to students about what is morally good and right in a critical and objective manner so that they can be able to form their own independent opinion on it when they grow up physically and intellectually. But all this can hold well only when we give certain minimal autonomy to students within our own conceptual framework of virtues. Teachers and school should neither indoctrinate nor impose their own intellectual and religious views on students which they entertain. They should rather allow students to sort out and choose their own intellectual views on moral and religious values. Moral virtues and religious virtues are not essentially contradictory to one another. But they may or may not go hand in hand because they rest on different premises. Moral virtues are not derived from nor do they rest on the belief in the existence of God from which most of religious virtues are derived. To cultivate a moral virtuous character one need not have any faith in religious dogmas because one can be morally virtuous without having any faith in any religion. But to say all this does not mean that to be morally virtuous one has to be non-religious. To be morally virtuous one need not be non-religious because moral virtues are not essentially opposed to religious virtues. Moral virtues are in fact included in most of our religious virtues. It only means that to be morally virtuous one has to give primacy to moral virtues over religious ones when there is a conflict between the two. The problem arises in imparting of moral education to students in multicultural societies like India only when moral educators and schools fail to distinguish moral virtues from religious ones and try to indoctrinate with their own religious values in students in the name of moral value education. There is no doubt about it that moral practices do differ from one culture to another. But it does not mean that different cultures do not share, nor can they share, any common moral principle. Common moral practices are found in different cultures simply because they share certain fundamental moral values underlying in them and these fundamental moral values we can say very well that they are secular and universal in nature. These moral values in Hinduism are called *sāmānya dharma*, which are not conditioned by the specificities of any particular culture, race, gender, caste or creed, etc., although, they originated from a Hindu culture. These values are meant for the goodness of everyone irrespective of their caste, creed, colour, etc. And such moral values, to my mind, can be very well taught to students and indoctrinated in them to make them to act virtuously as a good person acts, irrespective of their caste, culture or religion. For example, generosity, tolerance, truth, honesty, hospitality, sincerity, self-respect, self-sacrifice, diligence, dutifulness, kindness, brotherhood, love, etc., are universal and cross-cultural moral values and these values can be taught to students and indoctrinated in them in a neutral manner no matter which cultural, social and religious backgrounds they come, values are not contradictory to their specific religious beliefs and values are embedded in their respective religion and culture; they are common values; they are the very underpinnings of their religious and cultural life, and hence can be taught to students without any difficulty.

Thus, it is quite evident from the foregoing discussions that both the views mentioned above are extreme views, they are one-sided and hence suffer from certain shortcomings. The first view assumes that all individuals are rational, self-disciplined, enlightened and conscientious beings by making freedom as an essential component to be virtuous which is not the case for example, children. What to say of children, even most of us are not morally enlightened, self-disciplined, rational and conscientious beings who construct, rationalize and adhere to a moral code of one's own. We just follow the path of *mahājana*s of our own culture blindly because we believe that they were enlightened people; they had practical wisdom; whatever they have said that cannot be irrational and morally unjustified. Besides, it also assumes that no teachers, schools, governments have any moral right to control and interfere in the life of other individuals. Every teacher, citizen, school, government and society has certain moral duties and responsibilities, being a part of moral community, not only towards oneself but also towards other individuals in building up their character and making the society a civil society. To impart information about what is morally good and right to students does not necessarily mean to impose it on them. To indoctrinate certain fundamental moral values in students simply means to prepare them to act as a good person acts so that they can become a good citizen in future and this society also intends to achieve. Both these objectives we can achieve very well without discarding the moral postulate of human freedom, provided that we adopt a rational approach in imparting of value education to students and indoctrinating of certain fundamental moral values in them in a neutral and objective way. The problem arises only when we try to impose our own views or the views of some specific culture or religion on students. There is no doubt in it that moral values indoctrinated in students by teachers and schools at school level do not necessarily command their behaviour connection between the two. Not only this, it is also perfectly quite possible that students may value one thing and do another because there is no logical connection between valuing something and doing according to it. But these factors do not in any way, to my mind, imply that fundamental moral values should not be taught to students and indoctrinated in them at any cost, even if there are morally good reasons in doing of them. Further, empirical evidences clearly show that moral value indoctrinated in students does guide their conduct in most of the cases. The character and the conduct of *mahājana*s do have bearings on their life. The second view assumes that we can make people virtuous just by compelling them to act as a good person acts which not the case is because virtue is traits of character and traits of character cannot be created by making it legally obligatory. Virtue is a self-determined, self-governed, self-imposed, self-disciplined and self-cultivated habit. The moment when we try to create virtues in students by laws. Virtues loses their hold on them and created habits in them get lost when students move out from the school while virtues do not change so easily. The moral virtuous character does not change so easily simply because the cultivation of moral virtuous habits involve in them the role of one's own self. Building of a virtuous character always requires, to my mind, certain minimal sort of individual's autonomy. To say this does not mean that a moral virtuous character is an arbitrary cultivated habit. A moral virtuous character is not an arbitrary cultivated habit. It is a self-disciplined and self-cultivated habit and this habit is not formed by the individuals over night. The cultivation of a virtuous character always requires continuous conscious efforts on the part of the individuals throughout their life. But no virtuous character by itself makes any act virtuous. A virtuous character is only a habit or a mode of doing certain actions in a certain way whenever and wherever occasions arise within a society, and a habit or a mode of doing certain actions in a certain way whenever and wherever occasions arise is conceptually different from those what make it as a virtuous character. Obedience to authority does not generate any moral virtue by itself. Generosity is a moral virtue but giving things to people in order to avoid a penalty is not a generosity. To have traits like obedience and generosity is to act in accordance with one's own notions about the right and the good. A virtuous character results from virtuous conducts and virtuous conducts always depend upon the kinds of notions which we entertain about what is morally right and good within a society. From this point of view, we can say very well that moral virtues are relative to social environments. This implies that disposition to act in certain way is conceptually different from those that constitute one's character and both the things should not be muddled. Whether or not an action is virtuous depends partly on the reason for which it is done. The role of our moral educators and schools should always be only to present, propose and recommend certain moral values to students in a neutral and rational manner, but not to impose them upon students at the cost of their intellectual growth, creativity, wisdom, rationality and autonomy. When moral educators and schools adopt such kind of rational approach in imparting of moral value education to students and indoctrinating of certain fundamental universally upheld moral values in them, it helps students to develop good dispositions that enable them to flourish intellectually, individually, socially, and morally. The programme of character education does not, thus, simply mean a lesson or course on moral values. It is an integral part of our life.

# 3

# Rise of Education System and Its Moral Values

*Avinash Kumar Srivastava*

When even the sun of civilization was yet to dawn on the social psyche of the primitive savage and barbarian people, the education was playing its dominant role of training, transforming, informing and shaping the child's mind and behaviour for adapting and fitting them into the physical and social environment through appropriation of experiences of the elder or older generation. But before discussing the nature of primitive education it seems proper to clarify what does education means. The dictionary meaning of education is "to bring up, civilize, coach, counsel, cultivate, discipline, drill, edify, enlighten, guide, improve, inculcate, nurture, rear, school, teach, train, tutor, etc." When we cast our glance on the different meaning, interpretations and definitions of it we find that it has different sheds and meanings. For some education includes all the forces that influence the human development. For another set of scholars the connotation of education consists in teaching itself. John Stuart Mill, in his theatrical address presents the widest definition of education. He says

> "education includes whatever we do for our self, and whatever is done for us by others express purpose of bringing us nearer to the perfection of our nature, in its largest acceptation it comprehends even the indirect effects produced on character, and on the human faculties, by things of which the direct purposes are different; by laws, by forms of government, by the industrial arts, by mode of social life; nay, even by physical facts not dependent on human will; by climate, soil, and local position."[1]

But in his same speech he realized that this definition is too wide in nature and cannot be applied on the practical realities. Hence, be restricted it in the same address to the

> "culture which each generation purposely give other who are to be its successor in order to qualify them for at least keeping up and if possible for raising, the level of the improvement, which has been attained."[2]

The perusal of both the definitions of education gives in the Same speech, J.S. Mill points warden important fact, which is the idea of purpose, is invoked in the process of education. Second, if we happen to go through several definitions of education provided by different scholars we find that there are four important essential elements in the connotation of education. They are purpose, development, system, and knowledge or culture. In fact, purpose is involved in the very process of it, because for what education is imparted to a child. The reason may be to get them adjusted suitably in the society, circumstance and situation or for making him a good, noble or wealthy citizen. Without any purpose nothing can be perused including play and amusement. Thus, the idea of purpose is always felt to be essential in education. The second element is development. In the journey of education the skill and experience are automatically added in the compendium of information of a learner. It results in the development of ability and acumen of the student. Pestalozzi, a great educationist, has explained this idea through the metaphor of the tree. In his words,

> "sound education stands before me symbolized by a tree planted near fertilizing water. A little seed, which contains the design of the tree, its form and proportion, is placed in the soil. See how it germinates and expands into trunk, branches, leaves, flowers, and fruit! The whole tree is an uninterrupted chain of organic parts, the plan of which existed in its seed and root. Man is similar to the tree. In the newborn child are hidden those faculties which are to unfold during life."[3]

Education develops those faculties of a human being that hidden in the child in the seed form, Froebel, a loyal disciple of Pestalozzi, explaining his teacher's concept further adds,

> "So, the man must be viewed not as already become perfect. Not as fixed stationary, but as constant but as constant yet always progressively developing ... always advancing from one stage of development to another."[4]

Besides the idea of development and deliberate purpose, two additional elements are also present in the same form in the connotation of education, they are system and knowledge or culture. In certain sense a child is educated by the process of living, even when there is no visible purpose of educating him, and no system in the process; but insofar as education is treated as an art or as a science, it must be carried on with the deliberate purpose or modifying development by means of knowledge systematically imparted.

In this background if we cast our glance on the primitive society we find that the threads of education are very much present there, as when a child tries to situate himself suitably in the society he imitates the elders and improves himself by receiving insight and skill from the older generation. Unlike our modern complex society and its clumsy education system, wherein it is difficult to grasp its true nature, the primitive education and its system was in its simplest form. Here we do not find any school neither consciously recognized method of education, nor any method of examination or test or any teaching class. But despite the simple structure of primitive society and its indigenous method of education which instinctively, non-deliberately and unconsciously imparts the information, the essential characteristics of education and its system, are easily visible here. The reason is simple. In primitive tribes the old men were imparting the training to participate in their social activities, like religious ceremonies, festivals, and sacred occasions. This training was not in form of giving directions, or direct teaching to a child rather it was in form of imitation by the child of the elder's activity during any above-mentioned occasions.

## Nature of Education

Since in primitive society education was unrecognized, it appears difficult to explain its basic characteristics. However, the perusal of the daily routine of the society, costumes, marriages, and periodical festivity enables us to outline the essential features of their education that had been instrumental in child training or improving their physical and mental potentialities in meeting the problems of hand and hazards of the primitive life. Though there may be several part and processes of primitive training, broadly they may be divided into four sections. They are: 1. Practical Education, 2. Theoretic Education, 3. Value

Education, and 4. Teaching Class. Here, it seems proper to present their tentative description in brief.

## Practical Education

There is a famous saying that necessity is the mother of invention. It is true with the primitive educational method too. Besides play and amusement the process of obtaining food, clothing and shelter were instrumental in imparting the practical education to the primitive society. In fact, the life of primitive people was largely occupied with obtaining the above-mentioned three essential needs of the life. Children too accompanied the elders in their works and helped them up to their mental and physical calibre. In this process the children learnt the skill, through adaptation and imitation of adults, in procuring the life sustaining essentialities. This was an unorganized process of education that was provided to their children through their direct imitation of adults. Since children, in savage and barbarian societies always accompanied their parent or other elders of the family or society in their life sustaining ventures, the education there was a continuous process there. Because in doing so they not only imitated the adults, but also learnt through trial and error method too. The same is true in their amusement and games. The child plays with miniature imitation of the implements used by the adults. The boys shoot at the marks of bow and arrow, the girls make utensils of clay and play the preparation of food. Besides that there are a few simple games like ball and others wherein the child learns by imitating the adults.

Here, it seems proper to mention that it is not the case that all the training in primitive age was merely unconscious imitation, rather, latter on these culminated into conscious training or willful imitation. When boys and girls and assisted the adults in their life securing ventures or in play and amusements they have to learn them through conscious imitation, as either it is asked by the trainers or is the demand of the work. It is another thing that in both the cases the instruction on the part of the adult may not be the part of a conscious training or for the sake of educating the younger, rather it may be demanded for getting the work done or winning the game. But the child learn through conscious imitation. Now, with the rise of indigenous knowledge acquired through either trial and error method or through unconscious/conscious imitation, the primitive barbarian clans started training their children for cultivation, preparing small goods like pots and utensils and other things of clay, mat, fan, dishes, etc. from leaf or bamboo fibres. Thus, the process of passing over the skill and information from elders to younger generation continued, knowingly or unknowingly, consciously or unconsciously, either through imitation or through conscious narration, from generation-to-generation. Every generation added technique and skill earned through their own experience to the compendium of the knowledge. In this process human behaviour underwent refinement, addition and transformation slowly and stealthily. Despite all these, educating the child took place without taking a shape of education proper or systematic education process.

Finally, it can be said that the practical bearing of all the ceremonial activities, even, under the guardianship of the designated persons imparted them the art of capturing animals, art of making fire preparing food and similar processes of practical value. These may be said to be the process of education as all such practical activities had to be performed in a definite and stipulated way. And learning of all methods constitutes education.

## Theoretical Education

It consists in transmitting the younger generation the general body of knowledge or animistic beliefs which constitutes the interpretation of life experience. This aspect of primitive education is directly connected with ceremonies, dances and incantation. It was customary in the primitive society to perform such ceremonies or religious worship before starting some important or auspicious works like a military expedition, a hunt, planting the grains, harvesting, storing food grain or any other activity. In such ceremonies the younger generations were been continually instructed in the lore of the past. Initiation ceremonies are the glaring examples of theoretical education which possess special educational values. Men and women conduct this ceremony for boys and girls respectively. This initiation ceremony used to be a prerequisite for their admission into the adult membership of the tribe. These ceremonies were carried on in several steps and for a longer duration, often for several months or a year. Here the boy was painted on the body, tossed in the air, severely bitten and often mutilated. During this period, which last for few days, the youth is given a little or nothing to eat. By hunting he had to secure animals for the use in the ceremony. Here, he is trained to furnish food for adults. A guardian is always there to guide or instruct the boy. In some ceremonies the boy has to observe absolute silence, this ban is lifted by the priest or the medicine man who conducts this initiation. The rituals vary from one tribe to another but their dance and drumming as well as other tantrums are common bearing minor variations. During these ceremonies a child learns theoretic or practical lesions of life. In this process the education is imparted to the child consciously and in the real sense of the term, by an elder person, whether he is a priest or a medicine man or some trained elderly person.

Second, if we cast a glance on the life of primitive society we find that the life of the men is largely occupied in obtaining the necessities of life, i.e. food, clothing and shelter. And for procuring these they had to follow certain formal established methods, which were the outgrowth of the experiences of the past generations. The learning of these formal methods constitutes the most important part of education. The reason is simple. Its learning consists in becoming familiar with the results of the experiences of the past. And this part may be termed as the theoretic education. It is contrary to the immediate practical adjustment to the need of the environment which grows directly out of the individuals own experience.

## Rise of Values in Education

The perusal of previous lines hint towards the fact that amidst of the simple daily and complex practical and ritualistic routine of primitive men and their activities—social, religious and even the struggle for their existence—have inherent pedagogical importance. The reason is simple. Their activities mark a process of development in their skill, acumen and adaptation to the situation. At the same time this helped curtailing or refining the behaviour, like killing, looting, or torchering the other beings. It also cultivated some good qualities like singing, painting, helping, loving as well as policing the human behaviour to make them polite. And thus, the underdeveloped and unorganized primitive education strengthened their moral nature and enabled them to stand the tough and severest situations of life without being perturbed. This resulted in strengthening their moral fibre and prevented them from being affected by the wayward breezes of fleeting passions and prejudices. It has also been said in the closing paragraph with reference to the practical and theoretical education that there is an explicit consideration of the conditions or situations created to the development of knowledge and method of its transferring to the younger generation by the adults. This knowingly or unknowingly, willingly or unwillingly and slowly but stealthily the compendium of information, experience, and understanding kept continuously growing. And in this growth is hidden the rise of human values, social, religious, and normative. These are explicitly marked in the initiation ceremonies, where in it becomes apparent that there is a certain increase of purpose as well as socio-political, religious-ethical and practical values by properly observing them. A brief account of the value-related ceremonies and other tantrums, is needed here.

## Values that Stem Out of Initiation Ceremonies

The initiation ceremonies played a dominant role in inculcating social, religious and many other human values among the primitive youths silently. In this background if we cast our glance on the tribal initiation ceremonies we find that its activities have been instrumental in emergence of values. For instance through biting or mutilation of body a child or youth is taught to endure pain. Through exposure and want the child is taught to face the hardship and hunger. This radically resembles with *tapasa*, one of the *yama*s of *Yogasūtra*, which is a part of moral aspect of Yoga philosophy."[5]

> *Tapasa* means the strength of remaining unchanged in changes like that of heat and cold, hunger and thrust, standing and sitting, the absence of speech and the absence of social indication."[6]

## Emergence of Social Values

Obedience, discipline and to cater to the needs of the family or society are called social values. These values are also inculcated among the youths through the ceremonies. In other words it can be said that ceremonies are instrumental in getting the social values emerge among the younger generation taking part in these initiation ceremonies. In fact, certain ceremonies continue for a longer period where in the youth had to procure food either by hunting or through other means for the entire family. Here, he is expected to serve the elders as well as cater the needs of the family of which he becomes a member either through marriage or by adoption. This is meant for the purpose of continuing dominance of the elders in the control of the society. Thus, one of the most important virtue or value of life is obedience of the respect for the elders emanates from the performance of subservience. As through subservience to the performers they are taught obedience, and thus possess a social and political value too.

## The Totemic Symbol and Its Value

The totemic symbols that were painted on the body of men and women in any ceremony are also of pedagogical value, as they reveal history and tradition of a tribe. These transmit the message that their political, social order, science and religion all are in one.

> "The dance and ceremonial performances have similar purposes and are connected with their religious beliefs as well.... Their religious value is evidenced in the fact that the totem is the centre of worship and that the characters in these ceremonies represent totemic animals. Around such totems centre their religious myths. In explanation of these is found the fifth educational function."[7]

## Animism and Its Values

The animistic beliefs and its propagation among the tribal population by the elders and so-called priests to the younger generation was also instrumental in the emergence of normative values. In almost all the primitive tribes there was a tendency of interpreting the environment. While interpreting the animate and inanimate entities of the world they formed the belief that everything of this universe has consciousness similar to their own.[8] They named it soul, spirit or double. The reason is simple. The plain and simple mind of those savage people could not differentiate, for so many reasons, the difference between their own existence and the existence of other things of the world. The children were taught to obtain necessities of life without offending the spirit that dwells in every object they need. This gave rise to two different types of idea. The first is that everyone is equal as the same spirit dwells in all the things and beings of the world. Hence, we must have empathy for everything, animate or inanimate. Second, it gave birth to the seeds of deontological ethics instead of consequential one. Deontological ethical theory maintains that moral rightness or wrongness of any action dependents in its intrinsic quality and not on the nature of consequences, it holds that at least some acts are morally wrong in themselves.[9] "Deontological theories are often formulated in such a way that the rightness of an action consists in conforming to a moral rule."[10] The animistic beliefs, which were disseminated to the younger generation by the elders, carry the same spirit. Any action is right if it does not harm the soul dwelling in the things and beings of the world. The human action must confirm the basic principle of non-injury. Hence, one should inflict pain to others including birds, animals, and trees, hills, farms, water, and soil. This is an excellent example of normative principles of values that was inherent in the teaching and teaching system of primitive tribal society. It was reflected in every action of primitive man.

## The Teaching Class

In primitive society there were no teacher or teaching community, recognized or unrecognized. However, in normal course this role was unknowingly performed by the elders, parents or grand-parents as their work and activities were to supervise and guide the younger generation. Later on during initiation ceremonies and on other such occasions these supervision works were performed by the medicine man, the priest and others men and women. They created as well as perused ahead the mystical lore, tribal legend, wealth of story and proverbs to the new generation. And thus in the long run the teaching class came into existence due to the ceremonies too. The reason is simple. While the ceremonies were performed and participated by all men of certain group, yet they were under the direction of certain designated person. There additional work was to placate the spirit and obtain control over them through manipulation of symbols. Gradually, these designated persons started performing the role of teachers. Primarily, the so-called teaching class was made up of heads of the family groups; but as the duties of a father became more manifold and the worship became more complex, a special priesthood emerged whose work was to give formal, but elaborate instruction to the learners. And after certain interval of time such elderly persons of many uncivilized tribes invented and spread the art and culture. Later on they become the first professional teachers. For many centuries teaching remained the right of these clergy, but slowly but stealthily the primitive society developed into the earliest phase of civilization.

However, it will not be out of place to mention that

> "women played a dominant role as the mother, as the disseminator of so many forms of primitive culture, from ceramic art to the mysteries of religion, caused her, even in very remote age of human history to be thus spread, sometimes too when she was an apostle of the darker side of the knowledge, she was feared rather than loved for her skill and cunning."[11]

## Conclusion

It is clear from above discussion that primitive education was non-progressive and imitative in character. The younger generation learnt to live and meet the daily needs of life from the experience of the previous generation while seeking to adjust to the environment. Since, they were little conscious of the past as a form of life to be preserved or of the future as offering opportunities, they lived in the present and had a little tendency to change. Whatever change is marked in their skill and acumen, and way of living and experience, was accidental and unconscious. Coming to the age of teaching class or priesthood the interpretation of the life became more complex and ceremonies became so complex that the need to put them in permanent form was felt seriously. This gave rise to a written language and special subject matter of study came into existence. But these literary instructions were reserved to the priesthood alone. It consisted of directions of conducting worship and performance of rituals during initiation ceremonies and other festivities. So long education consisted of learning from elder generation to younger generation as what to do and how to do; the teaching method could not emerge. What remained there was learning through imitation. This situation of education existed for a longer period. But with the formation of teaching class in form of priesthood the written language came into existence and the subject matter for a higher stage of education came into existence. By that time the inquisitiveness also emerged among the primitive people. Rational explanation, as to how and why things should be done erupted, in the primitive mind. These were the sign and symptom of formation of a definite curriculum and the education was getting converted into a system comprising of teaching class and school in small and at local level. In this background the primitive society was entering into the early stage of civilization and education was converting into a formal system.

## NOTES

1. *Oxford Dictionary and Thessurus*, Vol. III, Oxford University Press, 5th reprint, 2006, p. 137.

2. Rectorial Address, St. Andrews, 1867, quoted from *Encyclopaedia of Religion and Ethics*, Vol. V, T&T Clark, Edinburgh, Charles Scribner's Sons, New York, 1965, p. 166.
3. *Ibid.*
4. *Ibid.* (Address on Birthday, Year, 1818) Menschenerrichung, Vienna, 1883, p. 16.
5. *Encyclopaedia of Religion and Ethics*, Vol. V, T&T Clark, Edinburgh, Charles Scribner's Sons, New York, 1964, p. 166.
6. *Tapa upavāsādina kāyaśoṣaṇam—Yogasiddhāntacandrikā*, p. 9, *Tapah śabden ... śarīraśoṣaṇam ca...—Yogapradīpikā*, p. 24: *Pātañjalayogapradīpa*, p. 275.
7. S.N. Dasgupta (1989). *A Study of Patanjali*, Motilal Banarsidass, New Delhi, p. 125.
8. Paul Monroe (1938). *A Brief Course in the History of Education,* The MacMillan Company, p. 84.
9. *Encyclopaedia of Religion and Ethics*, Vol. V, T&T Clark, Edinburgh., Charles Seribner's Sons, New York, 1964, p. 175.
10. Britannica, *Ready Reference Encyclopaedia*, 2006, Reprint, Vol. III, p. 138.
11. *Ibid.*

# 4

# Role of Education in Cultivation of Values

*Dhanpat Raj Bhandari*

There is a crisis of human values in our modern world. Ours is an age of paradoxes and age of alienation of men from his environment, the age of alienation of men from himself. Thus, we are passing through a phase in our life that poses a danger in the erosion of long expected human values. The goals of secularism, socialism, democracy, and ethics are coming under increasing strain. There exists schism between the formal system of education and cultural traditions. The preoccupation with modern technologies should not be allowed to sever our new generations from their roots in history and culture of nations. Deculturalization, dehumanization, and alienation must at all cost be avoided. Forces of social and national disintegration have become active, putting our democratic societies to severest test. The population increase has seriously affected the quality of life of the masses and has caused social tensions and unrest. Crime, violence, and indifference to human suffering are spread to all walks of life. Prejudices and complexes transmitted through the social environment and the accident of worth are hindering the promotion of equality. Our physical environment, viz., rivers, mountains, forests, plants, and animal life—is going increasingly polluted and depleted of its resources. This poses a serious threat to our quality of life. Narrow-mindedness and narrow-outlooks are dividing the people of this world and coming in the way of our developing a unifying national and international outlook. The world today faces a catastrophe threatened with global nuclear holocaust. As never before in the history of mankind, we are in need of peace and international understanding. All these problems cannot be effectively tackled through narrow piecemeal efforts, educational or social. What we need is drastic change in the very outlook of man in his own life values and his environment. This attitude will certainly make the development of human values in the New Millennium. Different cultures of the world have progressively eliminated many human values that previously used to provide meaning and purpose to human life. The economic and technological advancements that have taken place in the world have caused many serious problems and hence the turning back to search for human values in the New Millennium.

The values are the guiding principle of human culture. The growth and suitability of human society depends on and is sustained by certain essential values. Ethical, moral, social, and other values inculcated in the individuals are capable of guiding their behaviour to enable meaningful integration and the attainment of sustainable peace and orderliness. These are the values we should like to impart our modern youth for the development of human values in the New Millennium. In fact, the values referred to object, that we human beings cherish, desire, and consider desirable. This may be material things or abstract qualities and ideals like truth, happiness, and peace. Modern age is considered to be the age of Science and Technology and simultaneously, it is the age of crisis of human values because men have forgotten the importance of human values in their day-to-day life. Men have no time to stand and stare towards the human values, that is why the humanity is paving a pathway towards its catastrophe. Today our modern society is facing the problems of violence, crime, tensions, disintegrations, environmental pollution, nuclear catastrophe, population explosion, racism, communalism, bigotry and degradations of moral and human values. These problems are due to lack of right knowledge and right culturalization of the modern youth. The lack of value education is the primary cause and is an effective tool to counter them.

Man and values are inseparable. If man becomes stronger with education, the values, which brings forth wholeness to life and makes him the strongest. Education is regarded as a source of illumination, which brings to light the hidden potentialities, helps in harmonious development of personality and makes man capable of self-realization. Not only this, it is education which transforms biological man into a human being and a human being into a superhuman being. The process of education is based upon the conquest of knowledge over ignorance and that of virtues over evil. The process works through the eradication of polluting elements and inculcation of those values, virtues and qualities that help in truthful living. The prime concern of education is to evolve the good, the true and the divine in man so as to establish a moral life in the world. It should essentially make a man pious, perfect, and truthful. The welfare of humanity lies neither in scientific nor technological advancements and nor in acquisition of material comforts. It lies only in humanitarian education inculcating values in human beings.

The objectives of our education should be to turn out integrated personalities in whom have been inculcated noble ideals. In the importance of individual self-fulfilment, group cohesiveness, work and achievement as a fulfilment of one's duties. The main function of education is to enrich the character. What we need today more than anything else is moral leadership founded on courage, intellectual integrity and a sense of values. There is no substitute for a sense of values. Thus, we should try to see that the students should not only be intellectually competent and technically skilled, but also civilized in their emotions and refined in their purposes. Only then will they have liberal outlook, developed character and a respect for values.

It is observed that many ills that our world is suffering today, resulting in widespread disturbance and dislocation of life, are mainly due to the gradual disappearance of the hold of the basic principles of moral values in the heart of the people, and the only cure is in the deliberate inculcation of moral values from the early "years of our life". Again, it is observed that the weakening of the social and moral values in the younger generation is creating many serious social and ethical conflicts. It is, therefore, necessary and urgent to make our education value-oriented. Thus, the conscious and organized attempts be made for imparting education in social, moral, and spiritual values with the help of the ethical teachings of great religions. Therefore, our emphasis should be on the inclusion of the study of the great universal religions, on the rendering of social service to the community and participation in games, sports and hobbies and these will certainly contribute to the formation of right attitudes and values. As Coleridge rightly said, "Man may be made better not as a consequence of education but during the process of education". Hence, it is the process, which brings in charges through values. Dr. S. Radhakrishnan rightly commented, "A civilization is not built with bricks and mortar or steel and machinery, it is built with man, their quality and character".

The existing education system overall seems to be a failure in shaping the character of the youth. A continuous deterioration and fall in values can be observed in our youths and people of the country Kireet Joshi in *Perspective in Moral Education* (1995) aptly remarks,

> "Humanity today stands at a critical juncture. Hope and despair, pride and pessimism, comforts and confusion like human hearts in unequal and unstable measure. Whereas the peaks of material progress scaled by some countries, enthral humanity as a whole, the depth of social degeneration in most parts of the world make thinking people wonder, if mankind can receive the light of recovery at all."

The growing concern over the erosion of essential values and an increasing cynicism in society has brought to focus the need for readjustments in the curriculum in order to make education a forceful tool for the cultivation of social and moral values (observes the National Policy of Education, 1986). This is not the first time that concern has been expressed about the decline in the standards of moral and social life of our people and attention drawn to the rule of education in fostering a sense of values, but it has been deliberated on the different aspects of education by the several commissions. There can be no two opinions that education as an organized social system has an important function in the development of values. Nor can anyone deny that, we teachers, have a significant role to play in the realization of this objective. But if we are to be effective for the learning and cultivation of values in our youths through education, from the earlier stage of youth, then we are to make a complete review of our education system and develop a long-term plan to cultivate values among our youths.

Since education is a powerful instrument of social change and human progress, it is also a powerful tool to cultivate values in an individual. Therefore, all the educational institutes have greater responsibility to impart learning and cultivation of values through education. For inculcating values many educationists have suggested different ideas such as provision of value-based curriculum, designing special orientation programme for teachers, value-based foundation courses, publication of literature based on values, necessity to develop code of conduct for teachers and students, inculcation of philosophical view towards life among teachers and students. Further to cultivate values among the new generations we are to design a curriculum from out of our accumulated cultural heritage.

When we talk of learning and cultivation of values through education, we mean only that the development of proper values, attitudes, feelings and behaviour patterns which cut across all curricular experiences should be planned systematically and sincerely implemented. Our goal is "Education for Becoming" rather than the mere transmission of facts and information or the mechanical training of skills. We have to develop certain values as habits in the youths, such as cleanliness, punctuality and truthfulness. The rational understanding of values could be transferred to the stage when the youth is able to reason adequately. The youth should be made aware of the right values, to feel the proper emotions and internalize values in thought and deed. At the early stages value should be cultivated through concrete activities and life situations. At the later stages, the students should develop a rational understanding of the values and internalize them in thought and action. To be more precise, we can state that we can impart and cultivate values among the students and youths by developing the appropriate sensibilities —moral, aesthetic, cultural, spiritual values; by enabling the student to understand and appreciate the values of democracy, secularism, equality and scientific temper. The student should be enabled to develop a concern and commitment towards them; by providing opportunities for students to practice and live by these values.

Man exists not as a solitary individual living in a vacuum, but as an active member of dynamic social group, society, nation, and global community. The value education of a person should, therefore, be related to the specific social and cultural context in which he lives, and with reference to some universal and eternal standards applicable to all mankind. The NPE says:

> "In our culturally plural society, education should foster universal and eternal values oriented towards the unity and integration of our people. Such value education should help eliminate obscurantism, religious fanaticism, violence, superstition and fatalism. Apart from this combative role, education cultivating values has a profound positive content based on our heritage, national goals and universal perceptions. It should lay primary emphasis on this aspect."

The universal values which we have referred to above have been expressed in our constitution to which the Indian people as a whole owe allegiance, viz., liberty, equality, fraternity, democracy, socialism, and secularism. Apart from these values we would like our students to develop the values of protection of environment, equality of the sexes, removal of social barriers, scientific temper, international cooperation and peaceful coexistence, pursuit of excellence, equality and national integration.

Education for learning and cultivation of values can be provided directly, indirectly or incidentally. Direct education for cultivation of values among the students refer to deliberate, systematic instruction in values in specially provided periods in the school and college time table. In this approach, the values to be inculcated are explained, discussed and illustrated through stories and fables, anecdotes, moral dilemmas, real life events. Indirectly education can cultivate the values through the regular subjects of the curriculum and co-curricular activities. Education for cultivation of values is incidental wherever it is resorted to, in relation to specific events or situation that actually occurs in the educational institute. For example, an act of courage and bravery by a student, an act of indiscipline and moral failure, i.e., theft, dishonesty. The event may be one to be emulated or disparaged. Each approach has its strengths and weakness. They must be used judiciously always bearing in mind the maturity level of the learner and the interplay of head, heart, and will involve in the process of values-inculcation. The cumulative effect of these different kinds of experience both in and out of educational institute will lead to the internalization of the values and their realization in thought and deed.

# 5

# Values and the Universal Education

*D.R. Bhandari*

Education can achieve its ultimate purpose of making one an ideal human being, only if it helps fostering universal and eternal values in the minds of people. And for this, we must revolutionize our education, its means and ends. The meaningful education must not overlook any area of human development. So, the goal of education is not merely to produce good individual, but to turn our individuals, who understand their social responsibilities as integral elements of the society in which they live. Therefore, we can conclude that if education is to serve any meaningful purpose, the entire education system at all levels should be overhauled and restructured. The educationalists, intellectuals and scholars should come forward and evolve a sound, ethical and rational system of education which trains both the body and mind. We can say that the education should be value-oriented and not only academically oriented.

It is rightly said that the society will attain prosperity when it is managed by the people of high moral character, and this can be done only through providing value-education to its children. Education and values are closely related and the progress of a society totally depends on both. Education is a vehicle on which the norms and values of society are transmitted from generation to generation. Education can achieve its ultimate goal of making the members of society an ideal human being only if it helps in fostering universal and eternal values in the minds of all its people. Education is an integral part of the society which plays a greater part in forming good social order. The goal of education includes character building through development of such values as courage, discipline, compassion, fair-mindedness, firmness, truthfulness, patience, etc.

In fact, values are the guiding principle of human culture. Values means those desirable ideals which are intrinsic in themselves and are worthy of being pursued both from individual and social point of view. The growth, progress, and stability of human society depend on and is sustained by certain essential values. Values inculcated in the individuals are capable of guiding their behaviour to enable meaningful social integration and the attainment of peace and orderliness Our modern education system should now impart such values to the citizens. Broadly speaking, the objective of education should be all round development of human beings, and the attainment of higher life. And the moral qualities attained in the process of learning will be of greater significance for the life of individual and society. The modern society today is facing the problems of violence, crime, disintegrations, environmental pollution, and degradation of moral values, nuclear catastrophe, population explosion, racism, communalism, bigotry, etc. These problems are due to lack of value education which can counter them. Education, based on values has wonderful power to cope with the evils of the society and can give a progressive shape to the world. Education can have no significance, so long as it does not cultivate in the learner, an integrated outlook on life. Value-based education brings about the integration of the different entities of which the individuals are made of. Education proper makes a man complete. It should be moral and ethical based on high values like truth, non-violence, tolerance, and acceptance. We can rightly conclude that the destiny of a nation or society is determined by the generation of well informed, spiritually oriented, responsible and courageous citizens of ethics and culture. In this context we will be right to state that our educational philosophy should rest on the ancient Indian philosophical and cultural traditions with the higher goal of universal love and peace. The prime objective of education should be all-round development of human beings and the attainment of higher life.

Education in the modern context has two important components: "Value orientation" and "Vocationalization". Our educational programmes ought to be such that they provide adequate opportunities for each learner to develop him or her into a value-oriented person—socially responsible, humane, peace loving, dynamic and productive, to face and tackle the challenges in different walks of life. Value education takes up the challenging task of preparing the young learners to become morally sound, individually independent, and socially productive and responsible future citizens. Value education by developing individuals into productive workers will satisfy all their material needs in perfect harmony with higher values of life, facilitating the onward march of society to its ultimate goal of self-realization. Value education incorporates all the essential ideas of idealism, naturalism, humanism and pragmatism in a harmonious way.

Fortunately, the National Policy of Education 1986, underscores the importance of introducing value education in our school system. It says:

> "the growing concern over the erosion of essential values, and an increasing cynicism, in society has brought to focus the need for readjustment in the curriculum in order to make education forceful to the cultivation of social and moral values."

It again says:

> "in our culturally plural society, education should foster universal and eternal values oriented towards the unity and integrity of our people. Such value education should help eliminate obscurantism, religious favouritism, violence, superstition and fatalism."

It again says.

> "Deculturization, De-humanization and Alienation must be avoided at all costs. Education can and must bring about the fine synthesis between change- oriented technologies and continuity of cultural tradition."

The programme of value-oriented education must be taken seriously at the formal education level. The role of education functionaries like teachers and educational authorities seems to be very important. We need to sensitize the students of technical and professional education about the human and social significance of their chosen fields. Introduction of compulsory papers on value education may help in value orientation.

In our present era we are facing the value-crisis in human society and this can be met only by imparting value education to our present and future generation. We are in need of great efforts to implement this new approach. Of course, such organized endeavours have yet to go a long way to give the desired fruits of value education. Every responsible citizen of the society should accept this challenge and own responsibility in implementing a value-oriented lifestyle in the interest of our younger generations and peaceful progressive future of human society. "Discipline comes from within", said the great poet Milton. And this "discipline" can be fostered only by value-based education.

# 6

# Private "Public" Schools and the Right to Education

*Mahi Pal Singh*

Why do private schools, which are known as public schools in India, attract a large number of parents? We need to go deep into this aspect of education in our country particularly because Article 45 of the Constitution of India puts the onus of providing free and compulsory education up to the age of 14 on the state governments and the central government which run government (state) schools in states and territories under the direct rule of the central government. Failure of government run schools to artract students and to stop them from dropping out means that the government will never succeed in fulfilling its obligation under Article 45 and education to all children up to the age of 14 will always remain a dream as it had remained even after 55 yours of attatning freedom. Public schools cannot be expected to fulfil this aim as they are out of the reach of the general public even in metropolitan cities, not to speak of the deep and fur-flung areas of rural India where large sections of our sociery still fail to see the face of a primary school.

Admissions for K.G. and Nursery standards start with donations or payment under the table—amounts varying from ten thousand in one lakh and fifty thousand depending on the name and fame of the public school to which parents want to get there wards admitted. These schools charge heavy fees combined with compulsory purchases of uniforms, books and stationery from stores, which are run by these schools themselves or from pre-arranged stores. Except for the Board classes, these schools fix their own syllabi and prescribe their own books. Most of these books are those in which someone from a particular school has contributed as a writer and which are invariably priced very high.

Then start unit tests and their preparation—not by the teachers and their students, but by the parents of students. Since parents who send their wards to these schools are mostly businessmen are bureaucrats who have no time to look after their wards, and in most cases are not even trained to help their wards in studies, a search for tutors starts and the whole exercise ends up in arranging two or three tutors for every child. These tutors, most of whom are from government schools, shoulder the responsibility. Parents of those students who still do not do well are called once a month to the schools and there the teachers dutifully inform them of the failures of their wards. However, due care is taken about highlighting the abilities of their children. They are praised well to puff up the lungs of these parents, so that their middle-class sensibilities are not hurt. They rather have a sense of pride on being told that their children abound in inherent intelligence and talent.

However, if a child does not end up getting through the class at the end of the year, the parents are called and offered a "pass" certificate, along with an appropriate marks-statement for their children so that they can take their wards to some other school, which invariably is a government school. Thus, those not doing well are weaned away and extra payment-seats are created for new students to be admitted. Those, whose tutors work really hard, continue to produce better results adding to the name and fame of these schools. Some schools, not really well-known ones, provide certificates on payments ranging from five to ten thousand for other than Board classes even to those students who have not even seen their buildings, thus making extra money from this additional source also. Thousands of students with such (actually) fake certificates join government schools every year, as certificates of these financially unaided by the state, but recognized schools are fully valid for joining any school. Of course, some of the best students of government schools, whose parents feel that they should do something more for their talented children, shift to "public" schools every year. This continuous churning process ensures supply of better students, of course with better resources, to public schools and also impoverishing the already poor government schools. The net result is that there is a wide difference between their Board results. The different social strata to which the students of the two categories of schools belong is never taken into consideration while comparing their result, nor does anybody care about the abysmal difference in amenities available to the two categories of students.

An account of the state of things prevailing in government schools, written thirty-five years ago (*PUCL Bulletin*/ September 1990) by Dr R.M. Pal which says, "Even where schools function, the physical condition is deplorable—there are no desks, no drinking water facilities, no lavatories. You visit any corporation and government schools in Delhi and you find that children in primary sections are not provided with desks; they are required to squat. Children from poor families do deserve better physical environment than in their places of residence where they have no amenities of life. Let them have some amenities at least in their school where they can feel happy, and if they are happy they may not drop out", reads no different from another report, "No Drinking Water in 31 MCD Schools" published in the *Hindustan Times*, dated 31 August 2001 which stated,

> "The Municipal Corporation of Delhi is still unable to provide minimum facilities to its students in many primary schools. There is no drinking water provision in as many as 31 school sites. As a result, children have to fetch water either from their homes or slip out of the school in between classes to the nearest water tap. Of these, 13 sites are in Pahladpur Bangar Municipal ward in North Delhi, the other school sites are spread over Rohini, Shahdara (North) and Shahdara (South). Delhi Jal Board has been unable to provide tankers in these schools."

The account reads like a page of pre-Independence history of some remote area in Rajasthan and not that of what is happening in the heart of the capital of India after 75 years of achieving Independence, although the country is supposed to have made great technological advancement by developing Inter-Continental Ballistic Missiles (ICBMs) and nuclear arms capability during the last few years, which speaks volumes for the priorities of the government of the day. However, during the last few months, because of the intervention of the Delhi High Court as a result of a Public Interest Litigation (PIL) case, the local government has initiated some action to give government schools a better look at least outwardly, though much remains to be done if things are really to be changed, and if past experience is any indicator, nobody is serious about bringing about fundamental changes and improvements in the system and the conditions of education in government schools without which providing quality education to the vast masses of the Indian society cannot but remain a mere dream.

Unlike public schools, where teachers are selected and kept on rent, the government schools are stuffed with teachers, particularly the senior ones, most of whom do not even know their teaching subjects well. Government schools in Delhi prove the point best. Here Postgraduate Teachers (PGTs), called lecturers, who teach Senior Secondary classes, get promoted to the post in a queer manner. Trained Graduate Teachers (TGTs) teaching science or mathematics up to Secondary level are promoted as lecturers in any of the subjects in arts or commerce stream, like history, political science, geography, economics, sociology, accountancy, business studies and even in English, apart from mathematics, chemistry, physics and biology (which they teach in schools), only by doing a postgraduate degree course in that subject even though they do not study the particular subject during their graduation and have absolutely no experience of teaching that subject in their schools, whereas the rules do not permit TGTs of Hindi, Sanskrit, Punjabi, etc., to be considered for promotion in subjects other than these languages even though they generally study those subjects at under-graduate level and may have an experience of teaching such a subject for a long period in their schools with competence. The result, for example, is that many of the English PGTs themselves cannot write an application for leave and many PGTs in political science do not know the fundamentals of the Constitution of India. But who cares for these government schools?

Should the government and the officers responsible for perpetuating this state of affairs not be held responsible for criminal negligence of their duties and gross violation not only of Article 45 of the Constitution but also of the spirit of the fundamental human right to equality by denying to the students of government schools equality of opportunity on which the foundation of our Constitution, and in fact of any democratic society, is laid?

How serious is the then NDA government at the centre in providing free and compulsory education to all children up to the age of 14 years, is clear from the fact that even after passing the 93rd Constitution Amendment Bill (now 86th Constitution Amendment) in November 2001 making it a fundamental right of every child to get free and compulsory education up to the age of 14, it has failed to follow it up by a central legislation with a detailed mechanism necessary for its implementation even after a lapse of more than a year and a half. It was not unreasonable. Therefore, for the UNESCO in its "Education for All Global Monitoring Report: Is the World on Track", to include India in the list of 28 countries which in its opinion would not be able to achieve the target of universalization of primary education even by the year 2015. The reduction in the budgetary provision for education from Rs. 4,904.85 crore in the current year to Rs. 4,904.63 crore in the following year shows the government's apathy for mass education in the country. Its elitist bias is also clear from the fact that the Union government spends Rs. 39,000 per year for a student studying at a Navodaya Vidyalaya, whereas a student in an average government school gets only Rs. 2,000 including the central government's share of Rs. 241 ("Gross Neglect of Education" by Eduardo Faleiro, *Mainstream*, 29 March 2003).

The social welfare programme of providing free and compulsory education up to the age of 14 was not left to private "public" schools even by capitalist countries like Japan and the United Kingdom who bore the complete financial obligation needed to make it a success in the nineteenth century. How can we leave such an important obligation in the hands of purely business-minded people, for there are hardly any known educationists running these business establishments, who run these public schools for purely business reasons. However, if India has to stand in the line of developed countries this programme of universal education must succeed, because welfare of the country as a whole cannot be ensured without the well-being of its people, which in turn depends on their being educated, and educated well for that matter, because that is one of the essential conditions for a society to live a successful democratic life.

But it is my firm belief that these vestiges of the British Raj—the public schools—so long as they exist, will not allow the dream of universal compulsory education to be fulfilled because their very existence will hinder government schools from flourishing and shouldering this constitutional obligation, as they will remain a neglected lot so long as these public schools exist politicians, bureaucrats and the powerful middle-class people to send their wards to. The day they are all left with no option, but to send their sons and daughters to government schools, I am sure the government schools will be in a far better condition than these "public" schools, the breeding grounds of snobs who feel alighted in rubbing their shoulders with those of the sons of poor farmers, labourers, and those belonging to Scheduled Castes and Scheduled Tribes—in other words the sons of the soil of India, the real working class which can ensure the development of the country, and whose happiness and well-being in turn can be the only yardstick of measuring the development and prosperity of the country. These schools will become embodiments of equality and tolerance—the two cardinal values which are essential in a pluralistic society like India and which will make our society a humanistic and civilized society, devoid of the inequalities based on sex, caste, religion, language, and place of birth—the dream the founding fathers of our Constitution had cherished in their hearts and every civilized man will feel honoured to belong to. That will be a sure bet for ensuring development, security happiness, and peace in the country.

# 7

## Plight of Government Schools

### Who is Responsible?

*Mahi Pal Singh*

In the beginning of June every year when the results of the Central Board of Secondary Education (CBSE) are declared, an inevitable exercise of companion between government and public schools takes place, and the Delhi government, its Education Minister and the Directorate of Education announces schemes to improve the lot of government-owned schools. For a few weeks education officers, who are in charge of the 28 zones into which Delhi schools have been divided, start visiting schools. Meetings are held and reports are submitted, and after some fanfare everything again comes to its ever beaten path "normalcy" which is another name for apathy, negligence, and disinterestedness on the part of the Department of Education and also the Government of Delhi which has too many and more important duties to perform than to look after the education of poor people of resettlement colonies and *jhuggī* clusters and petty private and government employees who cannot dream of sending their children to public (i.e. private schools) schools, whose ever increasing demands of higher fees, building fund and donations even middle-class people are finding difficult to meet.

Education has remained the most neglected of subjects by coral and state governments in our country even after attaining political independence in 1947. That even the founding fathers of our Constitution did not assign to it the place of primacy it deserved in clear from the fact that they "did not make right to education a fundamental right guaranteed" by the Indian Constitution, and they put it in Article 45, under Part IV of the Constitution which is "non-enforceable" as it is entitled as the "Directive Principles of State Policy". But even the framers of the Constitution had made it obligatory for future governments to keep it in mind while framing their policies and to achieve the aim within a time frame of ten years. But these governments did not care to keep the Directive Principles in mind and never fulfilled their duty to provide "free and compulsory education" to all children "until they complete the age of fourteen" as envisaged under Article 45. This is in spite of the fact that the Preamble to the Constitution of India promised "to secure to all its citizens", "Justice—Social, Economic, and Political" and also "Equality of status and of opportunity" and our leaders are never tired of claiming our country as a "Socialist", to quote the Preamble again and "Welfare State". Successive governments remained guilty of criminal negligence to their duty towards the people of India ever since the adoption of the Constitution on 26 November 1949 by the Constituent Assembly, more so after 1993 when the Supreme Court of India declared the right to education, as granted under Article 45, a fundamental human right of every child in the country.

As two sets of schools developed in the country from the very beginning—public schools and government schools—the former for the wealthy elite and the latter for the toiling masses of the country, inequality in society became more pronounced —the development of two categories of citizens one of the rulers and the other of the ruled. The neo-rich, who reaped the fruits provided by the new culture of governance, which turned the rich into richer, and the corrupt into powerful, making a mockery of "equality of status and of opportunity", gave public schools every chance to flourish and the government schools to deteriorate further as the children of the new class of rulers did not go to this latter category of schools. As a result these schools were treated as an obligatory burden on the governments, because of the democratic pattern of our Constitution, to somehow exist for the sake of form only. It is not surprising, therefore, that the lot that these schools turn out every year forms the working class of the country, which children of poor parents and those belonging to Scheduled Castes and Scheduled Tribes were doing even without them. Government apathy towards government schools, public craze for public school education and patronage to public schools by politicians the ruling class, and the rich and well-to-do middle class leaves government schools a neglected lot. They are dumping grounds for children who have no better place to go. Most of these schools still lack basic amenities. They are manned by uninspired teachers, frustrated on many counts. There teachers who joined as Trained Graduate Teachers (TGT) after doing their PhDs and have retired or died without any promotion because the promotion rules are arbitrary, biased and irrationals. A Science or General TGT, for example, can get promotion as a Lecturer/Postgraduate Teacher (PGT) in any subject after doing an MA in that subject like history, political science, economics, sociology, commerce, accountancy, geography, maths, chemistry, physics, biology and many more subjects including English even if that teacher studied that subject for the first time at postgraduate level, and never taught that subject to students as a TGT, whereas language teachers/ TGTs in Hindi, Sanskrit, Punjabi, etc., cannot be promoted, except in that language, even though such teachers have been teaching that subject in the school along with their language or wholly because of the non-availability of the concerned teachers.

The Directorate of Education acts so arbitrarily that it did not promote eligible language teachers in other subjects, and other teachers in languages, even though recruitment rules for lecturers/PGTs were amended on 26 February 1996, which made it possible, and remained in force till 4 November 1999 when they were re-amended without being implemented for a day. Such things deny the guidance of teachers experienced in the teaching of, and capable of teaching, a particular subject to the students, whereas incapable and inexperienced teachers are thrust upon the helpless students. A Hindi TGT, one Ram Kishan Rohilla, who had been teaching English for the last 17 years, was not promoted as lecturer in English, and filed an OA in the Central Administrative Tribunal (CAT), Principal Bench which directed on 9 August 2000 that he should be promoted as lecturer in English. There are still thousands of such teachers in Delhi schools. Then, there are absolutely no promotional avenues for thousands of Yoga teachers, librarians, educational and vocational guidance counsellors and lab assistants. The result is that the Principal Bench of CAT has the highest number of cases pertaining to teachers of the Directorate of Education, Delhi because the Directorate has no time to listen to their problems. Hundreds of such teachers get more worried about redressing their grievances through the CAT instead of attending to their duties towards the students. What justice can such frustrated teachers do to the education of those entrusted to their care?

Then there are hundreds of contract teachers working in these schools, including Kashmiri migrants. The sword of retrenchment always hangs over their heads. They are neither regularized nor regular postings done in their places. On the one hand they are being exploited as they are not paid normal salaries, and on the other they block the promotions and appointments of those who have been in the queue for long periods of waiting. And what should students do in case even such teachers are not posted to their schools for years together? To cite just one example, Government Boys Senior Secondary School, Timarpur, just under the nose of the Directorate of Education, has been without the commerce and accountancy PGTs for the last very many years and the school Parent Teacher Association and the principal have written to the Deputy Director Education (North District) and the Directorate of Education so many times and the students have been appearing at the CBSE examinations year after year without having been taught a single word in these two subjects. Who is to be blamed if they fail to produce a result that should satisfy the officers of the Education Department and the Government of NCT of Delhi? Even the *Times of India* published an interview of the principal once in which he narrated everything, but even that did not break the slumber of the officials. And the Hon'ble Minister of Education, Government of Delhi has been issuing six-monthly statements that there are no vacancies in the schools whereas the Government of NCT of Delhi admitted before a division bench comprising Justice Anil Dev Singh and Justice O.P. Dwivedi of Delhi High Court, in the PIL filed by advocate Ashok Aggarwal on behalf of Social Jurists, on 19 June 2001 that as many as 4,000 posts of various categories were lying vacant in government and MCD schools including 730 of PGTs, 342 of assistant teachers, 454 of other category of teachers, 307 posts of vice-principals, and 229 posts of principals as on 31 December 2000 (as reported in the *Times of India* dated 20 June 2001). So much for the concern of the politicians and high officials of the Directorate of Education for the education of those going to government schools, whether primary or senior secondary schools.

Still it is only the teachers who are blamed for poor results in government schools.

# 8

# Gandhian Thought and Modern Indian Education

*D.R. Bhandari*

Education is a process of socialization, shaping and directing individual's personality development. The role and relevance of education have always been held significant since the dawn of civilization. It has also been accepted that it has a greater role not only in individual's development, but a medium for great social change. With its political and economic programmes, Gandhiji propounded a system of education, which might train both in science of man-making and social reconstruction.

What we have today in the name of education in modern India is the cancerous growth of "Macaulian Hierarchy", which is producing only clerks, engineers, doctors, and a fleet of white-collared servants, but no real and responsible citizens. In other words, we can say that education system in India, somehow or the other, is not egalitarian in character and form, but conservative in attitude and a product of "British Cultural Imperialism". Unfortunately, education has been equated with nearly acquiring academic qualification. Education has also been confused with literacy. That is why education has lost its utility and modern youths are getting lost. There is class distinction in Indian educational pattern, which is undesirable. We have "neglected mass education" and "given importance to class education". In this way, we are ignoring the need of rural areas. Our education pattern discriminates between the children of poor family and well-to-do families, between those who can afford full-time education and the working population. So long as class distinction and elite and sophisticated culture persists, the form and context of the present education system is not going to contain the forces of growing resentment. In fact, education today in India has become something of a status symbol. It promises job for the few people, but it is not true education because true education is one that makes people of character and high calibre.

There are three prominent aspects of the Indian educational system. First, it is ineffective and unproductive, second, it is elitist, third, it is monopolized in the hands of a small coterie of people. These three aspects are interrelated. Its elitist character both ignores the grassroot demands of productivity and produces a corrupt bureaucratic establishment. The official general view of education is paramedical, at the top of which, are the super- elitist institutions of higher learning and at the bottom is the pre-primary schools, in which the standard of school teachers are very low.

We are aware that primary education in India has been neglected and secondary education has already become a poor consumption product, and higher education is an instrument of elitism and cultural enslavement. It is the worst conceived inverted pyramid of our social system. The rural masses still remain as much in ignorance as in poverty. Gandhiji was of the firm opinion that polarization between the villages and the cities between those who do physical labour and those engaged in intellectual work, between the elite and masses, between the haves and the have nots and above all, between those who are more educated and those who are not educated, should not come about.

Gandhiji realized early the hollowness and insincerity of the educational policies of the British. He wanted to reform education in such a way that it should first feed the half starved millions, who are illiterate and helpless. Gandhiji denounced both the existing system of education and the class it has created. According to him the educational system has largely ignored everything that India had discovered in its educational experience, such as, children integrated with environment strong pupil-teacher relationship and identity with a pupil and an appreciation of Indian culture. The most devastating effect was the creation of a new class, i.e. an English-speaking class. Thus, we can conclude that basically his approach to education was national. As he wanted to present an alternative to the system introduced by the British in India.

## Aims and Objectives of Gandhian Educational Scheme

Gandhian educational scheme aimed at developing a spiritual man dedicated to truth and non-violence, but he was of firm opinion that this could be achieved only by working within and serving the society and not by withdrawing from it. Gandhiji stressed that the educational system must be one in which the highest development of mind and soul is possible. He believed in an integrated approach in which, the intellectual. The physical and the moral side of the child, right through his growth as a man, had to the property developed. Broadly speaking, Gandhi's educational philosophy and system can be described as "nationalist" in "setting", "idealist in arms" and "pragmatic in method" on the one hand, and "spiritual on the other".

Every educational system claims to aim at the highest development of the individual and at raising of man to a high moral and spiritual order, as well as, this becoming a useful member of society. The uniqueness of the contribution of Mahatma Gandhi is that he laid great emphasis on practice, i.e the practice of aims, objectives, principles, ideals, which must begin right at the beginning. He laid down a number of tests. First of all, he insisted that an educational system must be such that it can provide final answer to the poverty of India. Second, the educational system must cater to the needs of poor people living in villages by creating a productive base in the villages. Third, the various layers of education, from the basic to the highest, must aim at removing disparities and conflicts between villages and cities. Fourth, besides the aims of learning and productivity, the educational system must have the aim of imparting education of truth and non-violence. Fifth, higher education must inculcate in the adult, a national consciousness and his obligation to meet national necessities. Sixth, in Gandhian education system, the teacher occupies central place. Gandhiji says that imparting and receiving education is the most sacred duty of all and the teacher is the most sacred of men. Seventh, educational institutions must be viewed as communities linked with other communities in the society, through common endeavours and social achievement. Human perfection through education could be achieved only within the context of society and not by withdrawal from it.

Gandhiji contends that education should be "through life, for life, and throughout life". To construct a new society, it maintained the responsibility of education as enormous and held that old educational system cannot build-up a new society. Gandhian system of education prescribed pre-basic education for children, basic education for boys and girls, post-basic for adolescents, rural university education for the grown up students and adult education for workers and peasants. Gandhiji was of the opinion that mental and moral development and development of technology should not be divorced from each other. The productive work and learning should integrate. To create a Sarvodaya society, acquisition of learning through the process of productive work is essential.

## Basic Education

Gandhiji propounded in 1947, a system of education called Nai Talim. Literally, Nai Talim means New Education. It is learning by doing. Craft, art, health, and education were integrated in this scheme of education. Gandhiji held that it was a new method of education consistent with the conditions, obtaining in India predominantly made up of villages. According to him if education has to be linked with the living needs of the masses inhabiting the villages of India, it ought to be imparted through basic crafts. Nai Talim has two ends in view, first, all education be imparted on the line of crafts; and second, the produce of the crafts be made remunerative. He held that this system of education imparted through handicrafts was self-supporting and did not involve expenditure of millions on education.

Nowadays, students coming out of schools and colleges are mostly unemployed and are not able to find a way of earning their bread. "Tolstoy's bread labour was put into practice by Gandhiji in the *āśramas*. *Āśrama* means manual labour." The inmates of the *āśrama* had to win their bread by performing the manual labour and get their share by way of daily wages. It provided dignity of labour and an honest living for everyone, besides, the āśramites enjoyed a healthy life. About Nai Talim, Gandhiji himself said, by education I mean an all-round drawing out the best in child and man, body, mind, and spirit. This type of education was introduced mainly for the education of the children who fall between the age group of seven and fourteen. But, later on, Gandhiji held that this sort of education was necessary at all stage and for all persons including the university stage. We can summarize his scheme of basic education in K.G. Saiyidan's words that, what does Gandhiji actually postulate? First, that mass education should be made free, universal and compulsory, second, that this mass education should not be perfunctory, cut short at the end of four years, when the children have barely achieved literacy, third, that this education should be given through the mother tongue. Fourth, that this mass education should be given through village crafts like spinning and weaving and (not primarily) through books. That children should actually produce articles that are marketable and these should be sold to make education self-supporting.

Beside the theory of bread-labour, for which he contented that certain minimum physical effort on the part of everyone in society must begin at the beginning. He also suggested a totally different approach to the elementary education of children. He was for vocal rather than alphabetical training to begin with.

In India, there are a large number of scientific institutions and universities. Gandhiji openly approved the role of fundamental research and science and looked with great confidence at the marvels of science, but there is no use for science, which did not ultimately serve the interests of the people, particularly the elimination of poverty and the creation of equality. For Gandhiji technology was essentially an instrument of creating equality and bridging the gap between the haves and have nots. Although Gandhiji did not systematically develop his ideas about education, he made it very clear that oven at the level of higher education (colleges and universities). Educational institutions and industry must not merely be looked upon as two independent institutions, but both must be so integrated as to satisfy national necessities.

Therefore, Gandhiji concept of education cannot be separated from his other most important concept of *svadeśī.* What he was suggesting in Nai Talim or basic education, was the introduction of the concept of *svadeśī* at a very early stage. What he said about the integration of the industry at the higher education level was another aspect of a model of *svadeśī* economic development. It was his firm belief that without *svadeśī* there can be no national educational system.

Now, we come to the Gandhian view of the adult education, which also occupies important place in educational scheme of Mahatma Gandhi. Normally, adult education has come to be equated with the liquidation of illiteracy of those who missed proper schooling. In the Gandhain framework, this aspect is rather a minor part of the scheme. Adult education is the training of all men in filling the inevitable gap existing between early training and later requirements in the development of man's personality and values. There is always scope for new education in the context of the work one is doing. In India, where the masses remained uneducated and unskilled, the first attempt in adult education would surely require emphasis on literacy, but more importantly, it would mean continuous education in work, in fratenral cooperation, in service and above all in self-discipline. Therefore, to Gandhij□ adult education was a part of overall nation-building activity to fill the gap between the building of mental faculties and the structuring of the human personality.

Some educationalists doubt regarding Gandhiji's ideas about basic education. They say that basic education has been simply reduced to vocational training. But such doubts do not have any justification. Gandhiji himself had answered and clarified his position regarding the idea of basic education. In his own words,

> "Basic education is generally interpreted as education through craft. This is true to a certain extent, but, this is not the whole truth. The roots of Nai Talim go deeper. It is based on truth and non-violence in individual and collective life. Education is that which gives true freedom. Untruth and violence lead to bondage and can have no place in education."

Therefore, his theory of basic education cannot be ignored because the underlined ideas of his educational scheme were the same as those propounded for political and economic life. Gandhiji's ideas and concepts cannot be compartmentalized, nor can they be packed into different disciplines. They constitute one single whole and as such, apply to education as to any other human activity.

A question is often raised by some modern sociologists and other scholars regarding the efficacy of Nai Talim, that is, can Nai Talim be acceptable to the modern minds? There are some modern social thinkers who accept this sort of education including John Dewey, Stanley Hall and T.P. Manu who have also advocated and supported Nai Talim. According to them, this sort of education, if imparted, will be beneficial to all. It provides for an all round development of the individual. The head, heart and hands, all the three should harmoniously develop. Further, it is contended that Nai Talim or basic education provides for correlation of life. Certainly, there are some merits in this new system of education due to which Gandhiji introduced this scheme. The social thinkers like Vinoba Bhave and Jaya Prakash Narayan also accepted New Education scheme and tried to preach the Basic Principles of Nai Talim. We can conclude the scheme of National Education is suited to our needs. Requirements and genius and our aspirations for the future. It is for us to perfect it, it, and extend it, cover the entire field of education. In this process, adjustment and adaptation may be necessary, but these must be undertaken in the spirit of the total philosophy of Gandhiji for the individual and society.

# 9

# Philosophy and Education

## The Indian Perspective

*Y.V. Satyanarayana*

The word "philosophy" is derived from two Greek terms *philos* (love) and *sophia* (wisdom), which means love of knowledge and wisdom. Wisdom consists not only in the knowledge of things, but also in the evaluation of nature of things and appreciation of their value or worth. A philosopher wants to know the whole scheme of things and events in the universe with a view to understand the proper place of each thing in relation to the whole. Thus, the entire universe is included within the scope of philosophy.

The function of philosophy is to "order and guide" human life and action. It must advance and ennoble human life and broaden our outlook. Thus, philosophy is not merely confined to the pursuit of wisdom, but also a way of life. Since any philosophy arises and develops in the context of human life, it must take into account the contemporary social situation as well as the needs and aspirations of people.

Education is an essential ingredient of human life, for an uneducated person is considered as equal to a beast. It is education that makes a distinction between a man and a beast. Hence, the philosophers and thinkers of all ages and in all countries emphasized the value of education which enhances human qualities and suppresses brute qualities in man. Education has tremendous power to mould the attitudes, ideas, beliefs, values, and ideals of human beings. In other words, the success of humanity and its civilization, in all the ages, has been shaped and moulded by the educational philosophy of that period. Thus, education is a determining force in the creation of good persons and establishment of a better social order.

The philosophy of education is a branch of practical philosophy and it deals with the nature, content, forms, means, and aims of education for the intellectual and moral development of individuals. The ancient Indian and Greek philosophers developed systematic theories of education to carry out the educational requirements of people of their times, and to promote individual well-being and social harmony.

The ancient Indian thinkers visualized human life as a whole consisting of physical, psychic, and spiritual aspects. The progress of human society, as they thought, is not to be found in its material advancement, but to be found in what kind of people the society produces. The quality of life requires a balance between body, mind, and spiritual aspects of a person, and therefore, imparting of education is to be directed towards making the child into a whole person capable of leading a meaningful and purposive life.

According to ancient Indian thinkers, man is basically a spiritual being with a capacity to realize the spirituality. Man becomes completely human only when his sensibility to spirit is awakened.[1] To become human, one must realize his true and spiritual nature inherent in him. Thus, the ultimate goal of education, to Indian thinkers, is self-realization or knowing oneself, which means realization of the best qualities inherent in a person. Spiritual education does not mean teaching the irrational and dogmatic religious ideas, but acquiring the knowledge of inner self, awaken the student to this fact, enable him to find the spirit within and mould his or her life and action in the light and power of the inner self.

## Varṇa System or Social Gradation

The ancient Indian society has been divided into two systems of social organization—the *varṇa* (social gradation) and *āśrama* (stages of life). *Varṇa* and *āśrama* systems are basically social requirements for the good of the individual and society. The people are classified into four *varṇa*s or orders of the society[2] on the basis of their nature, ability, aptitudes, temperaments and capacities. The four orders are—brāhmaṇas (men of intelligence), kṣatriyas (men of ruling or warrior class), vaiśyas (men of business and agriculture) and śūdras (men of service who serve the other three orders). The division of society into four orders is a form of social division of labour, and the four orders looked after different functions of the society.

## Qualities and Duties of a Teacher

One of the primary duties of brāhmaṇas (men of intellectual class) is teaching to pupils. That man is called a brāhmaṇa (man of intelligence) who is engaged in studying and teaching, who strives for acquisition of knowledge, who is pure in behaviour and conversant with righteousness, who is always devoted to truth, who shows aversion for all unrighteous acts, and who controls his passions and propensities.

Since, the role of a teacher is very crucial in imparting education to students, the Indian philosophers accorded a special place or an elevated position in the society to the teachers. Of all the sections of the society, the teaching community enjoyed certain special privileges, because it is the teacher who shapes and moulds the future of the student. While the father and the mother are responsible for the birth and physical existence of the child, it is teacher who infuses life into the material body of the child by means of his knowledge and wisdom. For this reason, the Indian thinkers considered the father, the mother, and the teacher are equal to God.

For Indian thinkers, education is a process of unfolding or manifestation of the inherent qualities of a person that are present in him or her in a dormant state, or what Aristotle says actualization of one's innate abilities, talents and capacities to the fullest extent. In other words, education is a course of action that arouses or awakens the innate abilities, talents, skills and potentialities of a person, rather than imposing them from outside.

Swami Vivekananda says: "Education is a process of manifestation and perfection of those qualities that are inherent in the child." The duty of the teacher is to help and encourage the student for the manifestation of all the best qualities inherent in him. True education, for Gandhi, means drawing out of the best qualities inherent in the child.[3] It is the duty of the teacher to remove the obstacles and help the child to grow into a true human being. Thus, true education does not consist in forcing knowledge into the soul, but in bringing it out.

## Āśrama System or Stages of Life

The ancient Indian thinkers, unlike their Western counterparts, were not content with theorizing human life. They divided the whole life of an individual into four stages, and each stage of life is a training period in order to qualify himself for the next stage. At every stage the individual is supposed to discharge certain duties, and gradually evolve himself as a perfect being. Each stage is a progressive step in the life of the individual which finally leads him to self-realization.

The institution of *āśrama* or stages of life is a unique contribution of India to human ideals. The four stages of life are—*brahmacarya* (the stage of studentship), *gṛhastha* (the stage of a householder), *vānaprastha* (the stage of withdrawal from worldly life and going to forest), and *saṁnyāsa* (the stage of renunciation). Each stage signifies a place of halt in the journey of life to reach finally to the spiritual destination, that is, self-realization. At every stage the individual is supposed to discharge certain duties, and gradually evolve himself as a perfect being.

## The Stage of Studentship

*Brahmacarya* or the first stage of life is related to the life of studentship. It is the preparatory stage of the individual, and he is supposed to acquire the requisite abilities and potentialities to meet the challenges of life ahead, and the virtues that make him an ideal person. During the formative period of eight to ten years, the student is attached to a teacher. He should live with the teacher till he completes his studies, and serve the teacher like a menial servant.[4] His objectives are threefold—to acquire knowledge (both secular and sacred), to develop character, and to learn social responsibility.[5] He stays with his teacher and pursues learning as an end in itself, but not as a means to material gain. He submits to an austere discipline aimed at helping him conserve his energy and build a strong mind and body.

The student should cleanse his soul by purity of conduct and by restraints and vows. He should cast off procrastination and idleness. He should lead a life of celibacy and dutifully serve his preceptor. He should be ready to receive Vedic instructions, sitting at the feet of his preceptor, with eager desire to learn. He should cultivate simplicity, avoid evil speech, and take lessons only when his preceptor invites him for it.[6] Having thus passed the first stage of his life in the study of Vedas and observance of vows and fasts, and having given the preceptor the final fee, the student should take his leave and return home for entering into a life of householder.

After completion of studies, the student takes a bath symbolic of his studies being completed. The *Taittiriya Upaniṣad* describes a clear picture of the ancient Indian system of education.[7] The teacher instructs the student:

> "Speak the truth and practice virtue;
> Neglect not the study of Vedas,
> Not to be negligent of welfare and prosperity,
> Not to be negligent of duties to the gods and the fathers;
> Do not cut-off the thread of the offspring;
> Be one to whom the mother is a God;
> Be one to whom father is a God;
> Be one to whom the teacher is a God;
> Be one to whom the guest is a God;
> This is the command. This is the teaching.
> This is the secret doctrine of the Veda."

The ancient Indian and Greek philosophers recognized the importance of moral instruction to the young students to mould them into excellent and virtuous citizens. They thought that moral integrity is an indispensable prerequisite for the development of individual personality and for the establishment of a better social order. It is said that life without values is not a human life. The goodness or badness of a particular society depends on the conduct of men and women of that society. Hence, the ancient Indian thinkers regarded moral education as an essential requirement to every child and youth to lead a righteous and meaningful life ahead to them.

## Contemporary Trends in Indian Education

The concept of education in India has varied from time to time along with a change in social situation and a change in the needs and aspirations of people. Education, as one of the practical aspects of human social life, must cater to the needs and aspirations of people in their day-to-day life. Since education is one of the efficient means for material development, political evolution, and socio-economic progress, many new trends entered into the field of education to meet the challenges of the contemporary social situation.

True education must free one's mind from all the prejudices against the other men and make him realize the truth that every human being living in this world is akin to him. It should make every person to acquire the passion and perspective to fight against sexual and racial prejudices, class privileges, and group antagonisms. Since all human beings are born free and equal in dignity and rights, one must have regard for freedom, dignity and rights of others.

The modern men and women of India recognized the value of scientific and technological education to satisfy their material needs and comforts. Consequently, more emphasis is laid on scientific knowledge at the expense of ethics and aesthetics, literature and art, philosophical and spiritual knowledge which will contribute to the development of humanness in men. This trend in educational system has brought fast moral and spiritual degradation of people resulting in many social evils such as terrorism, violence, hatred, distrust, etc.

A proper synthesis of scientific and spiritual power could help the way for a better world to live in. To build a balanced personality, education should neither purely be materialistic nor purely be spiritualistic, but a combination of both, which is helpful in building a stable civilization. Too much stress on any one aspect makes education partial and unbalanced, and it may lead to cultural crisis.

Modern man should not regard himself as an Indian or American or European, but a human being that belongs to the whole of humanity. The purpose and goal of education must be directed towards establishing positive world peace. This goal can be achieved by inculcating an understanding and appreciation of other cultures in the young minds, and by establishing just and humane relationships among the people of the world.

## Concluding Remarks

Education enables individuals to develop into free and responsible citizens capable of self-determination. Education is a means to an end and that end should be creation of good persons and establishment of a better social order. It enlightens our insight and broadens our reasoning. Education is capable of establishing peace, progress, and universal brotherhood on earth.

Although Indian culture is basically spiritualistic in its outlook, the scientific and technological discoveries and their applications in modern times brought a tremendous change in the ideas, attitudes, beliefs, and values of contemporary Indians. Many contemporary thinkers believe that scientific and technological education is an essential requirement of the times to fight against the great evils of poverty, hunger, malnutrition, unemployment or to uplift the living standards of people. But at the same time spiritual education is also necessary to enhance the freedom, dignity, and rights of individuals.

The present generation in India and elsewhere is suffering from hatred, jealousy, anger, intolerance, distrust, dis-honesty, conflicts, violence, lust for power, etc. These evil forces are rampant everywhere and disturbing almost every aspect of human life. In order to set right the evil factors of our current social order and also towards creating a new world order, we have to emphasize the need for value-oriented education. The evil forces of contemporary social order are to be removed by appropriate educational instruction that can bring change in the heart and minds of young boys and girls. The youth have tremendous energy and vitality and it needs to be channelled in the right direction to get the best out of themselves.

To develop a strong character, we have to create a base for strong value system. To mould the character and personality of the child and the youth, value-oriented education must be introduced and taught at the school and college level to every child and youth. The course must be designed in a way that they reflect the ancient wisdom of India in a contemporary fashion.

Value-oriented education does not mean preaching certain religious and dogmatic ideas to students, but imparting the knowledge of universal values like truth, non-violence, tolerance, love, compassion, honesty, altruism, righteousness, universal brotherhood, global peace, etc. The contemporary Indian thinkers like Swami Vivekananda, Gandhi and many others emphasized the importance of value-oriented education as a remedy to many social evils that are disturbing the present humanity. Gandhi believes that strong character is the basis of a good citizen. Hence, he pleaded for instruction of value-oriented education to all young boys and girls along with other subjects. Swami Vivekananda says:

> "We need that type of education by which character is formed, strength of mind is increased, the intellect is expanded, and by which one can stand on one's own feet."[8]

Educational philosophy plays a vital role in the creation of good persons and a new world social order. It is an efficient and effective instrument for social change and development of a new world culture. The oneness of mankind should be the guiding principle of our educational system. Man's greatness is not in what he or she is, but in what he or she can be. The people of present generation, with free and untrammelled use of reason, are capable of finding solutions to their problems. Thus, the ultimate goal and purpose of our educational philosophy should be creation of good persons and establishment of an ideal world. Social order wherein the entire humanity can live in peace. prosperity and harmony.

## NOTES

1. Robert, A. McDermott (ed.) (1970). *Basic Writings of S. Radhakrishnan*, Bombay: Jaico Publishing House, p. 192.
2. The first reference to the fourfold division of *varna* system is found in a Ṛgvedic hymn known as Puruṣa-sūkta. (*Ṛgveda* X.90.12).
3. The Laws of Manu also refer to the fourfold division of *varṇa* to the divine origin (*Manu Saṁhitā*, I.87).
4. R.K. Prabu and U.R. Rao (ed.) (2002). *The Mind of Mahatma Gandhi*, Ahmedabad: Navajīvan Publishing House, p. 379.
5. In the Śānti Parva of *Mahābhārata*, in a discourse between the Sage Bhṛgu and the Sage Bharadvāja, the Sage Bhṛgu said. "In the days of Yore, the divine *Brahman*, for benefiting the world and for the protection of righteousness, indicated four modes of life." [*Mahābhārata*, English tr. Kisari Mohan Ganguli, New Delhi: Munshiram Manoharlal, 1981, Shanti Parva, Sec. CCXI, Vol. IX, p. 37.]
6. In the *Chāndogya Upaniṣad*, it is said that the pupil had to work for his teacher in house and field, attend to his sacred fires, look after the cattle and collect alms for him. (*Chāndogya Upaniṣad*, IV. 3, 5, and 10).
7. The *Dharmasūtras* of Gautama, Āpastamba. Vasiṣṭha and Baudhāyana contain regulations relating to social life and rules dealing with the duties of teachers and students. (*Gautama*, II. 14, 15, 20, 22 and 24; *Āpastamba*, 1.2).

   In later works like the *Pañcatantra* and the *Hitopadeśa* there were stories and fables which are meant for inculcation of moral truths. *Bṛhadāraṇyaka Upaniṣad*, III.1-4.

   *Taittirīya Upaniṣad* provides a clear description of the ethical teachings of the ancient Indian education. (*Taittirīya Upaniṣad*, 1.11.1-3).
8. Swami Vivekananda (1987). *Complete Works*, Vol. V, Calcutta: Advaita Ashrama, p. 342.

# 10

# Dimensions of Education

## A Gandhian Perspective

*Abha Singh*

Education is a life-long continuous human learning process. In its institutional form it is principally concerned with preservation of cultural continuity and transmission of knowledge to make the child civilized. But Indian schools tend to deny students the opportunity to think and act independently as the emphasis is on continuity of tradition rather than on spontaneity and creativity. Indian educational policies and programmes are apathetic to equip students in learning, how to take care of their emotional world, stay psychologically healthy and develop a wider perspective for making this world a safe place to live and enjoy life. The travesty of education is as rampant today as it was in the Gandhian age. Sensing its importance several hypothesis have been propounded on the nature of education. One of the more important ones is that of Gandhiji. In this chapter Gandhi's view on education has been brought under lens. For clarity and preciseness, I have divided the chapter in three parts. In Part I, I shall discuss Gandhi's ideas on education, wherein Gandhi's view of "Basic Education" would be discussed, and asses how far it would be effective. In Part II, I would dissect Gandhi's education system. In the process, I shall make assessment in the perspective of different dimensions of human personality, i.e., physical, intellectual, social and spiritual. In Part III, I shall make an appraisal on the issue under discussion and try to come to a definite conclusion regarding Gandhian perspective of education.

## I

The modernization of India started with the introduction of Macauley's education system. It opened the flood gate of knowledge and it acquainted the Indian mind with the culture of technology. The educational pattern, which was originally aimed at producing clerks for the proper functioning of the Raj, started producing visionaries who were committed to the idea of a rapid industrialization of India as well. But industrialization and technology are rooted in the idea that the life of comfort is the sole aim of existence. Although, Gandhi himself was the product of this pattern of education that tended to create a class of elites, Indian by birth but English by culture, but he had the insight to see the void created by it. He said, "it is my deliberate opinion that India is being ground down not under the English heel but under the modern civilization".[1] By modern civilization Gandhi meant the culture of technology. He further says,

> "Let us consider first what state of things is described by the word 'civilization'. Its true test lies in the fact that the people living in it make bodily welfare the object of life."[2]

Gandhi perhaps felt that in order to accommodate physical comfort one makes obliteration of social and moral values. It encourages the culture of value-neutrality and moral indifference. Therefore, Gandhi was keen to highlight the anomalies of English educational system and its role in the gradual erosion of values.

Gandhi's political thoughts are based upon the presumption that there is an element of essential goodness present in every man. It is only proper education that helps in bringing this element of goodness come to the surface. For him, the goal of education should be moral upliftment or character building and the cultivation of a conviction that one should forget everything selfish in working towards great aims.[3] Therefore, defining education Gandhi says, "By education I mean an all-round drawing out of the best in child and man—body, mind and spirit".[4] An all-round development of the mind can take place only when it develops *pari passu* with the education of the physical and spiritual faculties, which constitute an indivisible whole. Only such edcation is true. Therefore, it would be a fallacy to suppose that they can be developed piecemeal or independently of each other.

Gandhi was not in favour of an education that merely imparts instructions, or makes man literate. For him, literacy is not the end of education. It is only one of the means, whereby man and woman can be educated. Every individual is born with certain basic inborn tendencies and capabilities. The aim of education should be to bring out such inherent capacities of every individual. This would be possible only when theoretical imparting of instruction is combined with practical training. Hence, Gandhi postulated basic education which is meant to transform village children into model villagers. The object of basic education is the physical, intellectual and moral development of the children through the medium of a handicraft But it is not to neglect a very important moral principle, i.e., human labour and material should never be used in a wasteful or unproductive way. The emphasis laid on the principles of spending "every minute of one's life usefully" is best education for citizenship and that incidentally makes basic education self-sufficient. Gandhi observes,

> "We have up to now concentrated on stuffing children's minds with all kinds of information, without ever thinking of stimulating and developing them. Let us now cry a halt and concentrate on educating the child properly through manual work. Not as side activity, but as the prime means of intellectual training. You have to train the boys in one occupation or another, round this special occupation you will train up his mind, his body, his handwriting, his artistic sense, and so on. He will be master of craft he learns."[5]

It is clear from the facts, mentioned above, that Gandhi's "Basic Education" has far-reaching consequences:

> "It will bring the city-life and village-life closer and thus will eradicate the evil of class-difference. It will prevent the decay of village-culture and the lust for city-life, and thus will lay the foundation of a just social order giving equal opportunity and initiative to every individual. Moreover, as this system will make individuals skilled in their own arts, they will be masters of their own destiny, and will not become the object of exploitation of the privileged people."[6]

## II

On making a dent into Gandhi's ideas on education we find that it can be viewed in the perspective of four dimensions of human personality, i.e. (1) physical, (ii) intellectual, (iii) social, and (iv) spiritual.

### Physical

For Gandhi education was life-building, man-making and

character-building assimilation of ideas. All this would be possible on stout and healthy physical base since body is the first prerequisite of any development. Gandhi sadly noted that, on the one hand, millions of Indian students were undernourished and, on the other, government was apathetic towards the physical fitness of the mass. He strongly felt that the education system should be devised in such a way that it would help the child to achieve and inculcate self-confidence through healthy physical growth, concentration, chastity and by developing love for truth and love for fellow beings.

## Intellectual

Again, Gandhi felt that the intellectual dimension requires training of the mind in such a way that learning capacity of the student be stimulated. In other words, one must develop the capacity to learn. The clarity of thought is required to cope with information explosion. Special care must be taken regarding provision in our educational set-up for the adequate inculcation of the broad human values and outlook, especially in the science and technology courses. Science and technology itself inculcates no particular value. Still our lives are immensely affected by them, both positively and negatively. Hence, for Gandhi, educational system needs to be extremely cautious so that special provision is made to inculcate human outlook and values in the budding scientists and technocrats during the period of their training itself. It would prevent them being turned into mere automations. Similarly, the students of humanities and social sciences must not remain totally oblivious of the developments in science and technology, and they must have some suitable scientific and technological orientation. Additionally, students pursuing any discipline must be able to realize the basic assumption and implications of that particular branch in a truly philosophical sense. It would help one think critically and creatively.

## Social

Social dimension of education is no less important for Gandhi. He felt that no amount of mere individual development is sufficient to create a viable and dynamic society Man is essentially a social being and social values, if transmitted at an early stage through the educational system, would lead to a peaceful and integrated society. It was true in the Gandhian era as it is true today. In the age of unprecedented social turmoil and violence the last few decades have seen the emergence of vast sections of society which previously remained submerged. The old feudal basis of Indian society has collapsed and in its place new class and caste alignments have thrown national life into a continuing turmoil. Partially, it is good because an equitable social system can never emerge unless there is vast democratization of national consciousness. In all this turmoil the one fact that stands out starkly is the rapid erosion of what may be called moral or social values. The traditional value system has collapsed, but its place has not been taken by any viable alternative. Resultantly, the nation has been reduced to a moral wasteland, in which personal greed and sectarian interests take procedence over the larger social good. It is here that the English educational system has registered its greatest failure. Socially desirable values whether it is cleanliness or punctuality, discipline and teamwork, care or compassion, none of these find any place in the educational system adopted by us.

It is in this context that Gandhian ideas become more important, as it tends to instill in younger generation the attitudes of loyalty and devotion to the secular, civic and national values in social life and a sense of their priority over all other values in the social context including their priority over the values of denominational religion. Religion, for social and political purposes, must be taught to mean national morality touched with the emotion of holiness of the nation. The inculcation of this National value or *rāṣtra dharma* in and through education will enable one to realize in actual life the traditional Indian values of tolerance, accommodation and assimilation, on an operative basis. The supreme value of the individual as the ultimate unit of social and political life and organization, as enunciated by Gandhi, must be inculcated as the basis of all our educative process at all their stages. Our educational theorists and practitioners are required to work out details of programme in this regard. Such programme, developed in Gandhian perspective, would ensure that in the teaching of the democratic and socialist values a democratic balance between the rights and duties of the individual would be maintained. Such socialism would not denigrate into its totalitarian variety.

## Spiritual

Finally, for Gandhi, the spiritual dimension of any educational system is most fundamental. However, it is generally looked upon as the preserve of the individual or the family, rather than the educational system itself. It is true that under our constitution it is neither possible now desirable for the public education system to undertake religious education. Nonetheless, surely the system must at least provide some introduction to our vast and varied religious heritage in our zeal to preserve our "secularism" this dimension of human personality has plunged into oblivion. Herein lies the problem. What the system needs is to realize that the transcendent and religious have a peculiar held on the human mind and though they appear to have a tendency to develop the denominational and the exclusive still they have an appeal for the human mind which cannot be equalled in its strength by merely secular and moral. All religions are the vehicles of a broad moral and spiritual culture. They have a broad universal human appeal, providing for the cardinal elements and ways of human nature. It should, therefore, be possible for the educationist to devise ways and means to present and inculcate in the younger generations values of one's duty or *svadharma* through the use of this "religious" appeal without allowing its transmutation into the denominational exclusiveness of particular religion. Comparative study of purely ethical aspects of religions with a view to bringing about the realization of their essential unity are some of the educational means that could help indoctrinate in youth the balance between rights and duties.

## III

In nutshell, Gandhi devised his views on education in the traditional Indian pattern. But, he has never been allergic to new ideas. Never did he deny that Indian culture itself is the product of the intermixture of Aryan, non-Aryan, Hindu and Islamic ideas. It should be kept in mind that the introduction of English education in India exposed our people to the technological developments which were sweeping the West. But exclusive English education, devoid of value content, spoils human personality. Therefore, all the four dimensions of human personality, i.e., physical, intellectual, social, and spiritual, must be taken care of in the education of a child. As so, we have devised Gandhi's conception of education in view of four dimensions of human personality. All the dimensions, stated above, must simultaneously receive adequate attention if our educational system is to measure up tremendous challenges that we face today. Exclusive emphasis on any one of these to the others in an educational system would lead to perverse curriculum. Hence, social responsibility and social consciousness, which has been the ultimate aim of Gandhi, underlie all lofty values. It can be fostered, sustained and developed through education in its broad meaning, i.e., development of man's all round personality.

## NOTES

1. M.K. Gandhi, *Hind Swaraj in Collected Works of Mahatma Gandhi*, Chapter X, p. 24.
2. *Ibid.*, Chapter X, pp. 19-20.
3. B.K. Lal (1973). *Contemporary Indian Philosophy*, Motilal Banarsidass, 1st edition, p. 152.
4. *Harijan*, 31 July, 1937.
5. *Ibid.,* 18 September, 1937.
6. B.K. Lal (1973), *op. cit.,* pp. 154-55.

# 11

# Value Education
## A Critical Appraisal

*Sarita Kumari*

In the field of education, when we begin with any deliberation, it is becomes necessary to know or understand two questions; what are we going to study? And why this study is to be initiated? Second, does this deliberation have any worth, importance or aim related to the subject matter? The second question leads us to value education. Prior to discussing its subject matter, it seems proper to begin with a quotation of Edwin Mark Hani mentioned below:

> "We are blind until we see that in the human plan, nothing is worth the making if it does not make the man. Why build these cities glorious if man unbuilt goes? In vain we build the world, unless the builder also grows."

The above small quote indicates, very modestly toward the value education, which aims at the maximum development in the direction of total, as well as, all round upliftment or sublimation of human kind. But before going into the details of the subject matter, i.e., value education, it is an imperative on our part, to answer the "why" question mark related to it. In reply to it we can simply say, that there is a value crisis in the present world that has stooped or degraded down to its lowest level. It also needs to be discussed in the present chapter. In fact, value is a very broad term to which layers of meanings are associated. With the loss of value, human life is losing its merit very fast, for which the present consumeristic culture is greatly responsible. It has been contented by the scholars that "Value system and Morality are amorphous concepts". Time, place and social milieu are the chief departments of all the moral codes in the world. Morality, therefore, does lend itself to any precise interpretations. The world has enormously been changed. Old spiritualistic culture has been greatly replaced by the materialistic one. Science and technology explains the world through the law of causation, wherein nothing is beyond the chains of cause and effect, it appears that it is making a retreat towards the pagan world. In the words of Dr. Avinash Kumar Srivastava,

> "Science and technology have gained rapid pace. Economic boom and ban together have shaken the traditional roots of our pristine society. Chaos and confusion prevail in multi-directions that are the woe attitude, behaviour, thought and performance. New ethics seems to uproot the complete set of values."[1]

However, it is difficult to believe this retrogression and recoil of the evolution process, at the same time, it reminds of us Sri Aurobindo's theory of involution as an essential stage for completion of its cosmic cycle. This also indicates that our pristine values, virtues or moral codes that are being replaced today by a set of new one, may stage their comeback in the time to come, or in very remote future. We cannot rule out this possibility of their revival with a new naturalistic edifice, or interpretations, because there is a famous dictum "History repeats itself".

Here a question arises, what are the reasons that caused change or transformation in our ancient value system? In order to search its genuine answer, we will have to give a perusal of the social, political, religious and economic factors. The political state of colonized India exist more now and we have a democratic government today. In the economic arena, the old mercantile industries have been replaced by heavy industries. It requires heavy capital expenditure, good number of expert employees, artisans, technical experts, engineers and many other things. This implies concentration of capital in few hands bringing a deep gap between the have and have not's. This newly arising situation has dragged our society to a new problem of heavy strife between the labouring class and the capitalist. It is in fact, a new problem that was absent in our pristine society. In the social sphere, although caste system has legally been banned, but it has taken new *avatāra* (incarnations) in giving weightage in electing and selecting the candidates during elections, for forming a government. All these problems are new, but are far more complex and impede the fair vote system, because of the foul social systems of nepotism, caste bias and many others.

Now, the problem of having a clear and precise definition of value system is by no means simple. Here, it may be mentioned, that our moral values presuppose spiritual values too. But there is a difference between the two. In spiritual value, a greater stress and emphasis is given to the inner self of the individual and man's relation with the Supreme Being. Really speaking, individual exists at a microcosmic level, the Supreme Being on macrocosmic self. In a Sanskrit dictum, *yathā piṇḍe, tathā brahmāṇḍe*, both have been equated at par. Macro is not against the micro, nor is micro quite different from the macro, rather both are the same.

It appears proper to mention about a report prepared by a committee on "Religious and moral education", beaded by Sri Prakash, who defines moral behaviour as

> "Conduct of man towards man various stations in which human beings come together in home, social and economic fields and in the life of the outside world generally. Anything at helps to behave properly towards others is of moral value."[2]

It categorically indicates that the question of good or bad are socially constructed, depending on time, place and person, hence are relative terms. A dictum is often quoted "what is one man's meat others poison". This is a good example of relativity of "Good" or "Bad", depending upon three factors time, place and person as mentioned above. The same term good we bad depends also upon governmental laws. A reputed scholar has opened that

> "Though it is quite easy to discriminate between which is lawful and which is not, but there hardly any defined frontier between licit and illicit."

Normally, it is accepted that "morality" is concerned with belief and action both. It is in conformity with social norms that are shaped, modified and chiselled over longest span of time. Hence the two words, belief and action, becomes very significant in the field of ethics and morality. Sometime beliefs stressed upon by someone, individual or a nation and some time the action, due to the situational factor of that particular place, time and person. For example, the ancient Greece laid much of emphasis on the belief side of morality, on the other hand, the Indian seers were interested in translating the moral thoughts into the action. Hence here moral concept and precept both are important. This was the reason why our *ṛṣis* always asked to observe the moral code of conduct in thought, speech and action (*manasā, vācā, karmaṇā*). Another significant fact about the morality in India is that here the action part is so dominant that its observance is called *dharma*, the highest duty. In this sense Manu says *ācāraḥ paramo dharmaḥ śrutyukta smārta eva ca* in the same vain it is said *ahiṁsā paramo dharmraḥ*.

In Indian ethical-moral tradition there is a famous dictum *dharmasya tatvam nihitam guhāyām*. It means, that it is very difficult to decipher the real meaning or import of the ethical preachings. What is right or what is wrong, or what ought to be done and what ought not to be done, is difficult to be decided. The reason is simple, there is no commonly accepted objective definition of moral beliefs. It totally depends upon the intelligence and acumen of the agent, who is facing the moral dilemma. This is the reason the scriptures says, that in such a situation of indecisiveness, one should follow the footsteps of renowned wisemen of the place and time (*mahājana yena gatā sapanthā*). But the problem does not end here. The situation of confusion becomes worst confound, when one sees with eyes *ajara*, that belief and action go contrary to each other. For instance, adultery is immoral in very many countries, but in practice many renowned people are found committing adultery in broad day-light. Another example is that of several religious beliefs and customs that have no rational basis, are being observed by even the wise-people of the world. Vedas say at one place, *ahiṁsā paramo dharmaḥ* (non-violence is the highest virtue), but at another place, if prescribes cattle killing in the rituals of the *yajña*s. The rationale for it is given through a famous Vedic verse *vedikī hiṁsā hiṁsā na bhavati,* it means that the killing of cattles in Vedic *yajña's* ritual is not a violence. The examples are very many in the ancient scriptures and in everyday practical life. How can we interpret these situations and sayings of our scriptures? It is apparent from this discussion that there is an inherent problem in understanding the right belief, right action and moral code of conduct. Since morality is an abstract concept and is difficult to define, it can be understood by analysing and describing it in different forms and ways.

## NOTES

1. *Living Buddhism*, Avinash Kumar Srivastava, Patna: Impression Publication, 2011, Preface, p.v.
2. *Report of the Committee on Religious and Moral Instruction*, Union Ministry of Education, New Delhi, 1959, Para 30.

# 12

# Ethical Issues in Higher Education

*Yamini Sahay*

Two days ago we have come across a news informing us that the IAS trainees who made their reports during their training programmes had cheated and copied one another's so much so that every word to word matched in their reports. This made us astonished and compelled to rethink the ethical behaviour, rather ethical environment of the students as well as faculty in the campus. This is so because when such highly qualified incumbents can do such unethical wrongs what to speak of other general students studying in common disciplines (as science/arts) in schools and colleges. Apart from that technology has also enhanced plagiarism and other forms of academic dishonesty, and they have become growing concerns of campuses. Studies have shown that cheating is common among college students and that some forms, such as cheating on exams, have increased dramatically over the last three decades (McCabe, Trevino, & Butterfield, 2001).

Similar results are being reported from college-bound high school students. A recent study published by *Who's Who* among high school students indicated that 80 per cent of students who plan to attend college had cheated in high school. Most said they had never been caught and astonishingly, more than half did not consider cheating a serious transgression.

Some universities have implemented student honour codes thinking that in this way they could stem the rising tide of academic dishonesty. Birla Institute of Technology and Science, Pilani (BITS Pilani) is an example of a "modified honour code" that provides for strict penalties for dishonesty, but also has a strong educational component.

Studies suggest that honour codes can reduce academic dishonesty by conveying a consistent message to students that ethical behaviour is expected. They also promote students involvement in broader ethical issues. Thus, they help to create ethical campus communities. Apart from this, it has been seen that collegiate honour codes do have an enduring positive effect that extends beyond the educational environment.

So much so forth concerning ethical behaviour concerning students inside and outside the campus. But this is not all concerning the ethical issues in education. There has been degradations and ethical lapses in faculty also. Eschewing ethical responsibilities by teachers and professors are most common. In almost every nook and corner of campus one can find unethical actions by students, faculty other teaching/non-teaching staff. However, the problem is not worth describing in detail as it is known to all in public. Now, what should be done as part of solution to all these problems, is worth noting and so, this is the focus of the present chapter.

In the "Chronicle of Higher Education", De Russy (2003) asserted that "professional ethics begin on the college campus" (p.B.20), De Russy notes, and quite rightly, that colleges and universities must accept some of the responsibility for corporate scandals, because it is in college that many future accountants, lawyers, and other professionals receive their first exposure to ethical standards and traditions. Davis (2003-04) has also challenged those who control the academics to correct the "faculty organizational structures that enable irresponsible actions)" (p. 8).

Outlining further, the views of Davis, it would by worthy to mention that governing boards should establish clear standards for ethical behaviour. Not only this, they should ensure compliance with these standards, develop procedures to encourage honest scholarship and academic integrity, implement safeguards to ensure that faculty do not exploit their power relationships with students, and provide funding for ethics education.

## History of Ethics in Education

The call for universities to take ethics seriously is not new. More than two decades ago, the president of Harvard, Derek Bok felt the necessity for ethical temperament in education. Not to mention that he saw signs of degradation in ethical behaviour in students and faculty both, that he urged institutions of higher education to recommend to earlier academic traditions, the time when students moral development was considered an integral part of their mission (Bok, 1982). Bok regarded that the refusal of taking such responsibility not only violates its basic duty, but it also gives a filthy picture of moral indifference. To quote his words, when a university refuses to take this responsibility seriously, it "violates its basic obligations to society ... and gives an a impression of moral indifference" (p. 79).

Some universities have made policies that address standards of conduct for university officers and employees. But the situation, at least in India is the first of all not micro-planning in making these policies, have done, and second, whatever is reached in policymaking is seriously flouted, caring no one whatsoever. This is the case with some of the reputed institutions in India. An ethics policy that is required by state law should define ethical behaviour, and thenceforth compliance with laws and regulations. The ethics policy should reinforce state and federal mandates and other institutional policies that either require or prohibit certain activities such as affirmative action, nepotism, sexual harassment, and use of institutional funds for political purposes.

This is requisition on the one hand. On the other hand, research institutions should have endeavour and policies to promote ethical standards in the conduct of research and compliance with regulations regarding the use of federal research funds. Need there is specifically, that these policies are designed to minimize risk to human and animal research subjects, avoid conflicts of interest, and implement procedures for dealing with research misconduct.

There is no denying the fact that such policies are both necessary and useful. They not only help to ensure that a university functions within the law, but articulate important ethical principles. A bonus benefit turns out of this is that a good public image of an ethical institution is created. However, now, a is to be accepted, that most institutions give greater attention to establishing ethics related policies. Thus, they rarely venture, to evaluate how the policies are being implemented and whether they are achieving the intended results. Needless, however, it is to say that it also forms an integral part of the policy.

Information technology now practically made available to almost all research scholars, research studying has been very much affected. Now, mostly it is a hotch-potch amalgamation of many articles of the subject available online, so that it turns out to be less original. It is more of the nature of discussion and sometimes, inconclusive. The wisdom part of the research work is badly wanted so that it becomes imperative to encourage students that they construe informations into a wholesome knowledge and thereby construct important wisdom conducive to society. With regard to policies on research ethics, Frankel (2003) noted: "For all its scientific region, the research community has made little progress in assessing its efforts to promote research integrity." Frankel further said that such policies should be effective in nurturing an ethical research environment and reducing misconduct.

## Addressing the Ethical Issues on Campus

The institutions, whoever have made ethical policies for their employees and students, mostly focus on compliance. So, they offer limited guidance for "doing the right thing" in the broader sense of ensuring ethical learning environments, fulfilling the institutions responsibilities to the larger society, and informing faculty and other members of the campus community on ethical issues with respect to their relationships with students and each other. A search of the literature reveals several examples of initiatives that illustrate how universities are addressing these broader ethical responsibilities.

## Code of Ethics

In name of ethical policy adopted by different institutions. Variations we find assuming different standards. Varied codes are by and large connoted by ethical policy. Where code of ethics adopted by University of South California (USC) (2004) says, "We try to do what is right even when no one is watching us or compelling us to do the right thing". The Association of American Educators (AAE) in teaching students character qualities that will help evaluate the consequences of and accept the responsibility for their actions and choices. USC identifies ethical principles such as nurturing an environment of mutual respect and tolerance for diversity, attending to the well-being of students and others who are vulnerable, and distinguishing between behaviour that is ethical and that which is merely legal. It holds all members of the "Trojan family" students to trustees, responsible both for the ethics of their own behaviour and for building an ethical institution AAE while affirming strongly parents as the primary moral educators of their children, nevertheless believe all educators obligated to help foster civic virtues as integrity, diligence, responsibility, cooperation, loyalty, and respect for the law, for humans life, for others and for self. Quite at variance with this, the Florida Department of Education enumerates the code of ethics in the following way: The pursuit of truth, devotion to excellence, acquisition of knowledge, and the nurture of democratic citizenship. Essential to the achievement of these standards are the freedom to learn and to teach and the guarantee of equal opportunity for all. The educator's primary professional concern will always be for the student and for the development of the student's potential. The educator will therefore strive for professional growth and will seek to exercise the best professional judgement and integrity.

Codes of ethics also are used specifically to promote ethical teaching practices. These codes reflect the basic principle that teaching is an ethical undertaking. Though such initiatives as code of ethics laid out in detail encompassing every part of education is yet to be taken on a large scale by universities in India, a number of universities in Canada and some in United States have adopted "Ethical Principles in University Teaching" developed by a Canadian organization (Society for Teaching and Learning in Higher Education, 1996). The nine principles of ethical teaching outlined in the society's document include content competence, pedagogical competence, confidentiality, intellectual development of students, valid student assessment, dealing with sensitive topics, dual-role relationships with students, respect for colleagues, and respect for the institutions.

Apart from these, in addition, some universities have also adopted code of ethics to deal with certain business transactions. For example, Duke University was the first American University to develop a code of conduct for the companies it licenses to manufacture Duke apparel. More than 100 universities have followed Duke's lead.

However, even after coding the set of values, the ethical standard they want to pursue and follow, discrepancies are found between what they lay down explicitly and implicitly what they choose to do so. Thus, it becomes important that institutions of higher education pay attention not only to what they so but also to what they do. Giving a voice to this, UCLA professor, Alexander Astin suggested that universities often have two sets of moral values—these expressed explicitly in the institution's formal policies and pronouncements, and the implicit values that drive institutional practices with regard to matters such as allocation of resources, personnel decisions, curricular offerings, how the institution defines excellence, and the kind of assessment data it collects. Astin, further goes on to say that some of the most serious ethical problems in higher education arise from inconsistencies between an institution's explicit and implicit values.

## Ethics in Classroom and Beyond

As far as the central mission of higher education is concerned, it is to foster the intellectual and personal development of students. And, part of that responsibility is helping students develop a set of ethical standards to guide professional and personal decision making.

A recent report offers guidance for the more challenging task of producing graduates who are capable of ethical leadership and responsible citizenship. The young professionals who have prepared the report and published by Duke University's Kenan Ethics Programme rests itself on the promise that "...ultimate responsibility for the character of a democratic society rests with its citizens" (preface). Again, calling for principled leadership in all spheres of society, the report identifies several essential ethical principles, including mutual responsibility, working for the common good, transparency in business transactions, corporate social responsibility, integrating economic efficiency with environment sustainability, serving society's marginalized, commitment to community service, and the advancement of equality.

Scholars have even voted for service learning and other pedagogies that promote maximum student engagement in the learning process and say that they are more effective for teaching ethics than traditional modes of teaching. This argument seems particularly relevant to the task of preparing students to become responsible citizens and ethical leaders. As for example Fleckenstein emphasized that experiential learning can personalize and legitimize traditional classroom instruction by giving students opportunities to consider the broader social, economic, and political dimensions of ethical issues.

Saltmarsh noted that students often are taught to think about ethical decisions. But it is worth mentioning that it is only through the process of reflective enquiry and dialogue that they learn to recognize real life ethical issues and develop the commitment to make responsible choices. Therefore, Saltmarch recommended a process that he calls "connected knowing", both as a tool to teach ethics and as an ethical way to teach.

Institutions can provide a variety of opportunities for students and faculty to become engaged in ethics initiatives in the classroom and the larger community A few examples of such initiatives are as follows:

1. The Association for Practical and Professional Ethics (APPE) offers activities for students and faculty in conjunction with its annual meeting. These include a paper competition for undergraduates, a seminar for graduate students, and a National Intercollegiate Ethics Bowl, inspired by television's College Bowl.

Ethics Bowl teams prepare for debate on case studies representing ethical dilemmas on a wide range of issues, from academic integrity to professional ethics to social/political issues.

2. "A Matter of Ethics" is a national project spearheaded by the Association of College Honour Societies (ACHS) launched in 2004, the project encourages members of campus honour societies to work together to provide leadership for ethics programmes and activities. Project objectives include increasing campus awareness of ethical standards, promoting dialogue among student groups regarding ethical issues, strengthening commitment to ethical behaviour among peers, providing opportunities for ethical leadership, and increasing understanding of professional code of ethics within the various academic disciplines ("A Matter of Ethics", 2004).
3. The Centre for Academic Integrity (CAI), affiliated with Duke University's Kenan Institute for Ethics, provides a forum to affirm and promote the values of academic integrity. CAI defines it as "a commitment, even in the face of diversity, to five fundamental values: honesty, trust, fairness, respect, and responsibility...." (*Fundamental Values*, 1999, p. 4). CAI supports research and disseminates information about academic integrity, assists institutions in assessing the campus climate of academic integrity, provides professional development for faculty on academic integrity issues, and sponsors an annual conference for faculty and students.
4. Both public and private universities have established ethics centres to provide leadership for programmes and activities that support the study and teaching of ethics and contribute to an ethical campus community. A examination of websites for several leading

university- based ethics centres indicate that, although mission statements and goals vary, most seem to be broadly conceived to function as a resource for the entire campus community as well as the larger society. The website for the Rutland Centre for Ethics at Clemson University, for example, "states that it provides the campus and the community with a forum for exploration and discussion of ethical issues ... and serves as a resource for the people and the institutions of the state and region...." In addition, Cornell's *Programme on Ethics and Public Life* (2005) and the Lincoln Centre for Applied Ethics at Arizona state (2000) are examples.

## Implications for Faculty

To summarize all aforesaid, colleges and universities must take seriously their obligation to contribute to the moral development of students. Clearly, students will learn to "do the right thing" only within the context of an ethical institutions. Faculty and administrators in family and consumer sciences (FCS) and other academic disciplines have an important role to play in building institutions that promote integrity and practice it within the campus community and beyond. FCS professionals can and should:

1. Become informed about formal ethics related policies at institutions and initiate discussions about the effect of these policies on the creation of an ethical climate on campus.
2. Support the development of an institutional code of ethics that articulates core ethical principles.
3. Document inconsistencies that may exist between the explicit values communicated in written pronouncements and the implicit values that drive institutional decisions and actions.

4. Collaborate with colleagues to foster a campus climate that values diversity and ensures a welcoming, supportive environment for all.
5. Provide leadership to nurture an ethical learning environment that is inclusive, fair, and free from harassment and coercion.
6. Become informed about the social, political, and economic issues that have ethical implications for the profession. Ensure that FCS graduate and undergraduate students learn the principles and traditions required for ethical professional practice, as well as the knowledge and skills that will prepare them to become responsible citizens and ethical leaders in their communities.
7. Find ways to enhance opportunities for student engagement in experiential learning activities that provide exposure to real-life ethical issues.
8. Engage in national ethics initiatives, such as the Association of College Honour Societies project and in activities sponsored by the Association for Practical and Professional Ethics and the Centre for Academic Integrity.

## Include Ethics in Orientation Programmes

The above discussion leads us to conclude that ethical matters, whether large or small touch human lives at some level everyday. And there, the decisions which of ten are rendered without a great deal of conscious deliberation are perhaps illustrative of the implicit moral values discussed previously in this chapter. What is worthy of a closer more discriminating assessment is, the "implicitness" or perhaps ubiquity, of the moral frames that individuals apply to ethical judgement and behaviour. And this assessment may in fact, sometimes challenge the assumptions held by professionals in higher education about the moral and ethical maturity of their students.

Now, perhaps the time has come to stop assuming that most students arrive on college campuses with adequate foundations for ethical reasoning and decision making. So, as around the world in universities of reputation is being practised, apart from other things being done, considerable resources should be expended to address deficits in academic skills. In addition, some type of remedial education in reading, oral and written communication including math should also be provided.

Most institutions provide are require some variation of orientation for new students in order to provide important information about what their lives as students will be like, and to ease the transition. Academic ethics are and should be part of most college orientation programmes, but the primary focus is on what students know and understand about academic dishonesty, or cheating. Many students group that cheating is dishonesty, and it is dishonest to "copy" another student's work or exam paper, but fewer comprehend the ethical deficiencies and finer points of plagiarism. This lack of comprehension is a source of bemusement to faculty. And this bemusement, in turn, is sometimes a source of confusion for the students. In many cases, students involved in plagiarism or some other inappropriate use of another person's material genuinely are surprised to discover that work has been demand to be a product of cheating.

It is time to reconsider how academic honesty and broader ethical principles are understood by college students. Instead of assuming that students come to higher education hard-wired with ethical principles, colleges should expand and refine new students orientation programmes after first taking inventory of incoming students understanding and application of ethical issues and behaviour. Business frequently rely on ethical assessment tools as part of their human resource functions. If employee honesty is of particular strategic value to a company, human resource managers frequently are directed to include valid and reliable selection tests to measure a job candidate's ethical understanding and maturity. Some of these tools, appropriately modified, may be useful in assessing the same traits in new undergraduate and graduate students. If these tools consistently reveal a lack of ethical or moral maturity, the institution should then modify orientation programmes as well as other curricula to address the deficit. Likewise, it may be useful to assess the level of academic integrity and ethical understanding among faculty members. If such assessment reveals pervasive "inconsistencies between an institution's explicit and explicit (ethical) values" as discussed in this chapter, institutional leaders might consider requiring faculty and administrators to experience similar remedial ethical training and development. The institution then has role models for its students within the ranks of faculty and staff.

## REFERENCES


A Matter of Ethics (2004). *East Lansing, MI Association of College Honour Societies*. Retrieved from 9 July 2004, http://www.achsnail.org/ethics/index.asp

American Association of Family and Consumer Sciences (2003). Code of Ethics. Alexandria, VA: AAFCS.

Astin, A.W. (1989). "Moral Messages of the University." *Educational Record*, *70*(1): 22-25.

Association for Practical and Professional Ethics. (2004). Bloomington, In: Indiana University. Retrieved from 3 August 2004, from http://www.indiana.edu/-appe/program.html

Beht, G., Finch, M., Dobson, W. Abrams, S., & Brown, C. (Eds.), (1998). *The Content of Our Character. Voices of Generation X*. Durham, N.C. Duke University, Kenan Ethics Programme.

Bok, D. (1982). *Moral and Ethical Education in College: Theoretical and Practical Considerations. Beyond the Ivory Tower* (pp. 116-

35). Cambridge, MA: President and Fellows of Harward College. Reprinted by Josephson Institute on Ethics, Retrieved 29 May 2005, form http://www.academicintegrity.org.

Centre for Academic Integrity (2002). Durham, N.C. Duke University, Kenan Institute for Ethics. Retrieved from 29 May 2005, http://www.academicintegrity.org.

Colby, A. Ehrlich, T., Beaumont, E., & Stephens, J. (2003) "Educating Undergraduates for Responsible Citizenship." *Change*, *35*(6): 42-48.

Davis, G. (2003-2004). "Ethics: An Educational Imperative." *Community College Journal*, *74*(3): 6-9.

De Russy, C. (2003). "Professional Ethics Begin on the College Campus." *Chronicle of Higher Education*, *50*(4): B.20.

# 13

# Education and Swami Vivekananda

## A Quest of Life

*Kumkum Sinha*

In the literal meaning of the term "education" a man is to be regarded as a living entity with innate capacities and potentiality which are to be developed through education. Education means unfoldment of knowledge which is inherent in man, all knowledge is within man and not outside him. So, education means to develop that knowledge which is present in man's mind in vague form. "Education is defined as it is the manifestation of the perfection already in man."[1] Man possess every knowledge, but it requires an awakening. True education means an all-round cultural, physical, intellectual, moral, and spiritual development.

Education is not all about studying and getting good marks. It is really a means to discover new things which we don't know about and increase our knowledge. An educated person has the ability to differentiate between right and wrong or good and evil. It is the foremost responsibility of a society to educate its citizens. Vivekananda realizes that mankind is passing through a crisis. The tremendous emphasis on the scientific and mechanical ways of life is fast reducing man to the status of a machine. Moral and religious values are being undermined. The fundamental principles of civilization are being ignored. Conflicts of ideals, manners and habits are pervading the atmosphere. Disregard for everything old is the fashion of the day. Vivekananda seeks the solutions of all these social and global evils through education. With this end in view, he feels the dire need of awakening man to his spiritual self wherein, he thinks, lies the very purpose of education.

> "Education is not the amount of information that we put into your brain and runs not there, undigested, all your life. We must have life building, man making, character making assimilation of ideas. If you have assimilated five ideas and made them your life and character, you have more education than any man who has got by heart a whole library.... If education were identical with information, the libraries would be the greatest sages in the world and encyclopaedias the *ṛṣis*."[2]

Men are born in society (most of men). Education is a system that makes humans aware of the already existing and prevailing structures and systems that govern or used to govern the lives of men. And zeitgeist, too. So, students learn language, history, science, mathematics, arts and crafts, logic, medicine, economics, etc. All these teachings of these subjects and likewise should make students aware of the reality around them and make them understand that they are a part of a larger community, something greater than themselves. So, when students learn these already existing structures and patterns in nature and men, they can create something new, something which might prove to be simpler than its ancestor, more comfortable to men, or simply, aesthetically pleasing. Or, if they choose not to create something new, they might simply exist for the existence of the system.

In the beginning there was a system of *guru-śīṣya* tradition, to obtain knowledge one has to go to the *guru—yaha tana viṣa kī belarī guru amṛta kī khāna, śīśa diye jo guru mile to bhī sastā jāna.*[3] The verse of Kabīr Dās which is full of the importance of the *guru* who is the backbone of our culture, describing the body as a poisonous plant and the *guru* a reservoir of the *amṛta*, it can only be achieved by bowing our head in the feet of our *guru.* This was the only source to attain knowledge. But now the time has changed, at that time *gurujī*, who was a centre of veneration, was considered good enough. There were disciplines and values were always kept in mind, they are the eternal values, i.e. truth, *ahiṁsā*, non-acquisition (*aparigraha*), respect for religious persons, etc. During the last couple of hundred years, however new values have emerged equality, liberty, democracy, secularism, etc.

There are two categories of knowledge, declares the *ṛṣī* of *Muṇḍaka Upaniṣad*—knowledge of the world and knowledge of the inner world, material knowledge (*apara-vidyā*) and spiritual knowledge (*para-vidyā*). The same thing has again been taken up in the *Chāndogya Upaniṣad* by sage Nārada Muni and Sanatkumāra. In fact, both ought to be acquired and both are equally important. Nor are they mutually exclusive. One is incomplete without the other. This has been very strongly shemphasized by the *Īśa Upaniṣad.*

"The higher (*para*) and the lower knowledge (*apara*), or the knowledge of the spirit and the knowledge of matter, both ought to be acquired, so say those who know *Brahman* (Supreme Spirit)",[4] declared the Sage Aṅgirasa to Śaunaka when the latter approached him as a disciple. All the Vedas, grammar, philosophy, astronomy, astrology, and all such knowledge falls in the category of *apara* or lower learning. That knowledge by which *Brahman* (Supreme Soul) is known, that by which, the unseen and the unknown, the one eternal all-pervasive Being is known, is the *para* or higher learning.

*Guru* is one who gives *vidyā*. *Śikṣaka* gives *śikṣā*. *Vidyā* teaches morality, values, difference between good and bad, etc. *Śikṣa* teaches subjects meaning math, sciences, languages, and social sciences, etc. The *guru* also taught how to lead a life with *dharma* (virtues).

In the Prākṛt literature, we get a beautiful education—"Education ought to achieve two objects—(1) To solve the problem of livelihood. (2) To attain *sadgati,* i.e. to develop the values of life or values promoting good conduct." In the absence of the above-said values, it is not possible to awaken the "good" in human nature, to construct a healthy society. In Jaina Ideology, we get indication of two kinds of education—(1) *Grahaṇa śikṣa*—Theoretical knowledge, (2) *Āsevana śikṣa*—Practical knowledge The former is the knowledge gained from the *guru* or a teacher or a treatise, while the later is the applied knowledge gained by putting into practice the former one. Although, in today's scientific field, the second type of education is going on, yet the practical training for bringing about these desired transformation in the consciousness (at mental and emotional levels) is lacking even there. For the development of the values promoting good conduct and behaviour, it is necessary to regulate/balance the *cetanā* (consciousness), especially at subconscious or unconscious level. To fulfil this we have developed a system of "Science of Living" under the auspices of Late Ācārya Śrī Tulsī, the Founder of the Aṇuvrata. The Yogic postures (*yogāsana*), breathing exercise (*prāṇāyāma*), perceptive meditation (*prekṣā dhyāna*), relaxation exercise (*kāyotsarga*) together with self-awareness, auto-suggestion and contemplation (*bhāvanā, anuprekṣā*) comprise the strategy of the science of living, the practical exercises of all these are to be done for the transformation of consciousness. This practice is useful for the students of science as for those of the arts faculty.

The current education system, the way I see its end results, has grown to be capitalistic in nature, rather than the holistic and altruistic traditional way. With the rise of industrialism and colonialism and slavery through hands of Europe, in particular, men grew to be lesser reverent of nature and community, and rather pursued goals of self-interest. As Adam Smith says, in wealth of nations, when every individual tries to make best personal gains, he ends up uplifting society, too. But, in the end, it is all Zero Sum Game, isn't it? (Nash Equilibrium) So, the current education system, the one I am a part of, is seen as a means to a comfortable and less risky lifestyle. Which, in a sense is a good statement to make! But, it is not complete. Even though that is what the system must be saying, what I have learnt from my teachers through my school years, is that, they want me to succeed. They want me to have money, they want me to have a house, a car, a prestige. Which all, when you grow to understand selflessness, seems self-centred. Man cannot be irreverent. Part of humanity, we all are, and capitalism is not the ultimate answer to this.

Science is the ultimate enquiry in nature and how things work. Even though with all the uncertainties of knowledge and the madness, science in the end stands on hard evidences and pure empirical reasoning. "Science is selective system of cognitive orientation towards reality". Science makes our lives less miserable and more comfortable and more enjoyable and longer, may be. Other than getting lost in the madness and extreme beauty of uncertainty, there are no as such limitations of pure science.

The education system in India, as audited and taken from British dossiers, summing it all up says that educational institutions were pretty perfectly established throughout India. Children were taught science, medicine, arts and crafts, history, language, logic, and etc. And the system including the caste-system, and Indian society, as a whole, sustained and flourished through centuries, with emperors and families coming and going. I find myself unable to comment on education in India before British, but, if education were to be equated with lesser ignorance, the way I imagine it, people had grown to have the fear of non-acceptance and fear of failure. And, those fears still persist. Without the urge of knowing things, people got along with the system, because it worked.

With this background Swami Vivekananda appears on the scene in India with a different opinion. Education is nothing but "the manifestation of perfection already in man".[5] In the literal meaning of the term "education" a man is to be regarded as a living entity with innate capacities and potentiality which are to be developed through education. This notion about the nature of human being is essential so that education can be carried on. Swami Vivekananda observes,

> "Whatever a man knows should in strict psychological language be what he discovers or unveils. What a man 'learns' is really what he discovers by taking the cover off his soul."[6]

Each soul is potentially divine, and the goal is to manifest this divine within. It aims at man-making, life building, character-making. The end and aim of education is not theoretical knowledge, but the unfoldment of the entire potentialities of a man.

Swami Vivekananda stressed on giving the public only positive education, because negative thoughts weaken men. Swami Vivekananda told, if young boys and girls are encouraged and are not unnecessarily criticized all the time, they are bound to improve in time.

In New York, Vivekananda used to observe the Irish colonists come—downtrodden, haggard-looking, destitute of all possessions at home, penniless, and wooden-headed—with their only belongings, a stick and a bundle of rags hanging at the end of it, fright in their steps, alarm in their eyes. Vivekananda observed a completely different spectacle in next six months—the man walks upright, his attire is changed. In his eyes and steps there is no more fright. Swami Vivekananda tried to find out the cause, he told, if this incidence is seen by the explanations of Vedānta, that Irishman was kept surrounded by contempt in his own country—the whole of nature was telling him with one voice—"Pat, you have no more hope, you were born a slave and will remain so". Having been thus told from his birth, Pat started believing in it and hypnotized himself that he is very low. While no sooner had he landed on America than the shout went up on all sided—"Pat, you are a man as we are, it is man who has done all, a man like you and me can do everything, have courage!" Pat raised his head and saw, that it was so, the self-confidence within him woke up again. Swami Vivekananda feels likewise, the education that young boys and girls receive is very negative. He thinks they do not gain confidence or self-respect from these education, so according to Swami Vivekananda only positive education should be given to children.

## Objectives of Education

Vivekananda points out that the defect of the present-day education is that it has no definite goal to pursue. A sculptor has a clear idea about what he wants to shape out of the marble block; similarly, a painter knows what he is going to paint. But a teacher, he says, has no clear idea about the goal of his teaching. Swamiji attempts to establish, through his words and deeds, that the end of all education is man making. He prepares the scheme of this man-making education in the light of his overall philosophy of Vedānta. According to Vedānta, the essence of man lies in his soul, which he possesses in addition to his body and mind. In true with this philosophy, Swamiji defines education as "the manifestation of the perfection already in man". The aim of education is to manifest in our lives the perfection, which is the very nature of our inner self. This perfection is the realization of the infinite power which resides in everything and every-where—existence, consciousness, and bliss (*satcidānanda*). After understanding the essential nature of this perfection, we should identify it with our inner self. For achieving this, one will have to eliminate one's ego, ignorance and all other false identification, which stand in the way. Meditation, fortified by moral purity and passion for truth, helps man to leave behind the body, the senses, the ego and all other non-self-elements, which are perishable. He thus realizes his immortal divine self, which is of the nature of infinite existence, infinite knowledge, and infinite bliss.

At this stage, man becomes aware of his self as identical with all other selves of the universe, i.e. different selves as manifestations of the same self. Hence, education, in Vivekananda's sense, enables one to comprehend one's self within as the self everywhere. The essential unity of the entire universe is realized through education. Accordingly, man-making for Swamiji stands for rousing mans to the awareness of his true self. However, education thus signified does not point towards the development of the soul in isolation from body and mind. We have to remember that basis of Swamiji's philosophy is Advaita which preaches unity in diversity. Therefore, man-making for him means a harmonious development of the body, mind, and soul.

In his scheme of education, Swamiji lays great stress on physical health because a sound mind resides in a sound body. He often quotes the Upaniṣadic dictum *nāyamātmā balahīnena labhyaḥ*; i.e. "the self cannot be realized by the physically weak". However, along with physical culture, he harps on the need of paying special attention to the culture of the mind. According to Swamiji, the mind of the students has to he controlled and trained through meditation, concentration and practice of ethical purity. All success in any line of work, he emphasizes, is the result of the power of concentration. By way of illustration, he mentions that the chemist in the laboratory concentrates all the powers of his mind and brings them into one focus—the elements to be analysed and finds out their secrets. Concentration, which necessarily implies detachment from other things, constitutes a part of *brahmacarya*, which is one of the guiding mottos of his scheme of education. *Brahmacarya*, in a nutshell, stands for the practice of self-control for securing harmony of the impulses. By his philosophy of education, Swamiji thus brings it home that education is not a mere accumulation of information, but a comprehensive training for life. To quote him: "Education is not the amount of information that is put into your brain and runs riot there undigested, all your life." Education for him means that process by which character is formed, strength of mind is increased, and intellect is sharpened, as a result of which one can stand on one's own feet.

Education plays a vital role in liberating women from the society, Swami Vivekananda had held Indian women in high esteem and has appreciated their typical Indian features like spirit of service, compassion, affection, contentment and reverence. Swami Vivekananda felt that no nation can grow without taking care of the interest of women. He said,

> "All nations have attained greatness by paying proper respect to women. That country and that nation which does not respect women have never become great, nor will ever be in future."

He felt that Indian women must be given the liberty to live an independent life. They must have the right to take decisions and, when faced with problems, should learn to solve it themselves. The only interference that can be made is while providing proper education and making them aware of the society. He felt education of women is the only tool to move forward, and a medium which could help to eradicate all grave problems and help to make them the ideal women in the world. There may be problems in between, none can be so serious that cannot be solved by the magic word "education". He felt that Indian women had a good understanding about chastity, because it is their heritage. So, it was important to intensify that ideal within them and then all aspect would fall in place. He said women, apart from knowledge about science and art, should be given training about religion, hygiene, and cooking, sewing and other simple works of life. Swamiji wished the ancient *śraddhā* to return as a remedy to solve the problems of women and change the parental attitude that somehow they have to dispose of a girl to marriage when she be of age.

Vivekananda, in his scheme of education, meticulously includes all those studies, which are necessary for the all-around development of the body, mind and soul of the individual. These studies can be brought under the broad heads of physical culture, aesthetics, classics, language, religion, science and technology. According to Swamiji, the cultural values of the country should form an integral part of the curriculum of education. The culture of India has its roots in her spiritual values. The time-tested values are to be imbibed in the thoughts and lives of the students through the study of the classics like *Rāmāyaṇa, Mahābhārata, Gītā,* Vedas and Upaniṣads. This will keep the perennial flow of our spiritual values into the world culture.

Education, according to Swamiji, remains incomplete without the teaching of aesthetics or fine arts. He cites Japan as an example of how the combination of art and utility can make a nation great. Swamiji reiterates that religion is the innermost core of education. However, by religion, he does not mean any particular kind of it but its essential character, which is the realization of the divinity already in man. He reminds us time and again that religion does not consist in dogmas or creeds or any set of rituals. To be religious for him means leading life in such a way that we manifest our higher nature, truth, goodness and beauty, in our thoughts, words, and deeds. All impulses, thoughts, and actions which lead one towards this goal are naturally ennobling and harmonizing, and are ethical and moral in the truest sense. It is in this context that Swamiji's idea of religion, as the basis of education should be understood. We note that in his interpretation, religion and education share the identity of purpose.

Why religion forms the very foundation of education becomes clear in his following words:

> "In building up character, in making for everything that is good and great, in bringing peace to others, and peace to one's own self, religion is the highest motive power, and, therefore, ought to be studied from that standpoint."

Swamiji believes that if education with its religious core can invigorate man's faith in his divine nature and the infinite potentialities of the human soul, it is sure to help man become strong, yet tolerant and sympathetic. It will also help man to extend his love and goodwill beyond the communal, national, and racial barriers.

It is a misinterpretation of Vivekananda's philosophy of education to think that he has overemphasized the role of spiritual development to the utter neglect of the material side Vivekananda, in his plan for the regeneration of India, repeatedly presses the need for the eradication of poverty, unemployment and ignorance. He says, we need technical education and all else which may develop industries, so that men, instead of seeking for service, may earn enough to provide for themselves, and save something against a rainy day. He feels it necessary that India should take from the Western nations all that is good in their civilization. However, just like a person, every nation has its individuality, which should not be destroyed. The individuality of India lies in her spiritual culture. Hence in Swamiji's view, for the development of a balanced nation, we have to combine the dynamism and scientific attitude of the West with the spirituality of our country. The entire educational programme should be so planned that it equips the youth to contribute to the material progress of the country as well as to maintaining the supreme worth of India's spiritual heritage.

The Vedic period is said to be of complete equality for women. Then came the feudal period, foreign invasions which took away women's freedom, and the national movement against foreign domination, which also took women's rights and equality as important along with other issues. Swami Vivekananda has been very vocal about the emancipation of women all through his life. In post-Independent India, even though there has been noticeable rise in the activities directed towards women's emancipation, most of the women in the rural areas are illiterate and trapped in a vicious circle of poverty and deprivation. It is, therefore realized that the women have to be provided with the vital educational inputs, if they are to become a powerful force in the society, and participate in the developmental and decision- making process.

Girls are brought up only to marry someone and not develop as a fully productive citizen. Through educating the masses this situation should change. Swami Vivekananda's philosophies and contributions towards the women society shall always be remembered for generations to come.

Swami Vivekananda is one of the most admired spiritual leaders of India. The world knows him as an inspiring Hindu monk, his motherland regards him as the patriot saint of modern India. Among the modern Indian reformers and leaders, who stood for complete equality of men and women, the most outstanding was Swami Vivekananda. He was highly sympathetic towards the oppressed position of Indian women and argued for gender equality. It is the Hindu culture and the Vedānta philosophy on which Vivekananda's position on women is based. According to Vedānta philosophy, men and women and all beings are divine in their essential nature. In the modern times, the history of women shows that they have come across many changing statuses.

Finally, I can conclude with some of his point as following:

> "Education is the manifestation of perfection already in man." He said that education which does not enable a person to stand on his own feet, does not teach him self-confidence and self-respect, is useless. Education should be man-making, life giving and character-building. He also said that children should be given "positive education", i.e. they should be encouraged to learn new things till they gain self-confidence and self-respect.

**Of Religion**, Vivekananda said "To be good and to do good unto others—that is the essence of Religion". According to Swami Vivekananda, religion is the idea which raises the brute to man, and man unto God. Swami Vivekananda preached that truth is the basis of all religions and hence we must always practice tolerance towards other religions—be it Hinduism, Buddhism, Christianity, Islam or other Religion.

**On Character**, Since a country's future depends on its people, Vivekananda stressed on character building (he called it "man-making"). According to Vivekananda, *jīva* is Śiva (every man is potentially Divine). To become divine (or great), man must give up suspicion, jealousy, conceit and learn to work unitedly for the common good. Courage, faith (in oneself and in God), patience and steady work, according to Swami Vivekananda, is the way to success. He told that purity, patience and perseverance overcome all obstacles.

**Womanhood**, Swami Vivekananda said that since the *ātman* (soul) has neither sex nor caste, it is wrong to discriminate between sexes. He suggested not to think of people as men and women, but as human beings. According to Vivekananda, there is no chance for welfare in the world unless the condition of woman is improved. He felt that it was impossible to get back India's lost pride and honour unless the condition of women was improved. According to

Vivekananda, the ideal of womanhood in India is motherhood and that Sītā was the ideal of Indian womanhood.

**Hinduism**, Vivekananda strived to give to Hinduism a clear-cut identity, both nationally and internationally. At the end of the nineteenth century, the Western world knew very little about India. The British masters and Christian missionaries had conveyed to them the picture of a barbaric, backward race of people practising evil and inhuman Hindu customs. Moreover, the Hindus in India were practising many different customs and traditions and were a loose confederation of many different sects. Swami approached the problem in two parts. Within India, he preached about the common bases of Hinduism, the common ground of all its different sects and brought about its overall unification. He also toured the Western countries in an effort to convey Hinduism's liberal and universal values to Westerners and raising his voice in its defence. He also worked among the masses fighting social evils and superstitions and trying to integrate the best elements of Western culture into Hindu culture.

**Regarding Spirit of Service**, Vivekananda said:

> "Do not stand on a high pedestal and take five cents in your hand and say, 'Here, my poor man', but be grateful that the poor man is there so that by making a gift to him, you are able to help yourself. It is not the receiver that is blessed, but it is the giver."

Another saying

> "Believe in the omnipotent power of love. Who cares for these tinsel puffs of name? Have you love?— You are omnipotent. Are you perfectly unselfish? If so, you are irresistible. It is character that pays everywhere. Give up jealousy and conceit. Learn to work unitedly for others That is the great need of our country."[7]

**National Integration**. Swamiji said that in spite of innumerable linguistic, ethnic, historical, and regional diversities; India has always had a strong sense of cultural unity and has been one nation. Swamiji strived to instil in Indians, a greater understanding of their country's profound spiritual heritage and pride in their past. He undertook tours to different parts of India and gave public speeches to rouse religious consciousness and to focus the attention of educated people on the plight of the downtrodden masses. He urged them to work for their emancipation, saying:

> "So long as the millions live in hunger and ignorance, I hold every man a traitor who, having been educated at their expense, pays not the least heed to them."

At this stage, man becomes aware of his self as identical with all other selves of the universe, i.e. different selves as manifestations of the same self. Hence education, in Vivekananda's sense, enables one to comprehend one's self within as the self everywhere. The essential unity of the entire universe is realized through education. Accordingly, man-making for Swamiji stands for rousing *manas* to the awareness of his true self. However, education thus signified does not point towards the development of the soul in isolation from body and mind. We have to remember that basis of Swamiji's philosophy is Advaita which preaches unity in diversity. Therefore, man-making for him means a harmonious development of the body, mind, and soul.

Having analysed the goal or objective of education, the next question that naturally arises is about the method of imparting education. Here again, we note the Vedāntic foundation of Swamiji's theory. According to him, knowledge is inherent in every man's soul. What we mean when we say that a man "knows" is only what he "discovers" by taking the cover off his own soul. Consequently, he draws our attention to the fact that the task of the teacher is only to help the child to manifest its knowledge by removing the obstacles in its way. In his words:

> "Thus Vedānta says that within man is all knowledge even in a boy it is so and it requires only an awakening and that much is the work of a teacher."

To drive his point home, he refers to the growth of a plant. Just as in the case of a plant, one cannot do anything more than supplying it with water, air and manure while it grows from within its own nature, so is the case with a human child. Vivekananda's method of education resembles the heuristic method of the modern educationists. In this system, the teacher invokes the spirit of inquiry in the pupil who is supposed to find out things for himself under the bias-free guidance of the teacher.

Swamiji lays a lot of emphasis on the environment at home and school for the proper growth of the child. The parents as well as the teachers should inspire the child by the way they live their lives. Swamiji recommends the old institution of *gurukula* living with the preceptor and similar systems for the purpose. In such systems, the students can have the ideal character of the teacher constantly before them, which serves as the role model to follow.

Although Swamiji is of the opinion that mother tongue is the right medium for social or mass education, he prescribes the learning of English and Sanskrit also. While English is necessary for mastering Western science and technology, Sanskrit leads one into the depths of our vast store of classics. The implication is that if language does not remain the privilege of a small class of people, social unity will march forward unhampered.

We can understand him in his own words:

> "Education, Education, Education alone! Travelling through many cities of Europe and observing in them the comforts and education of even the poor people, there was brought to my mind the state of our poor people, and I used to shed tears. What made the difference? Education was the answer I got. Through education comes faith in one own self, and through faith in one's own self the inherent *Brahman* is waking up in them, while the *Brahman* in us is gradually becoming dormant."[8]

Thus, we see that Swami Vivekananda was in favour of securing proper balance between the well-developed body, mind and soul, for true education firm foundation is to be built-up first and this foundation is ultimately spiritual. The ideal or object of education is therefore not theoretical but practical, it unveils the hidden treasure in man and kindles the light within him.

Swami Vivekananda stressed on different aspects of religion, youth, education, faith, character building as well as social issues pertaining to India. Vivekananda was a Hindu monk from India who played significant role in introducing Vedānta to the Western world and also reviving and redefining certain aspect of the religion within India. Rabindranath Tagore commented about Swami Vivekananda and his teachings, "If you want to know India, study Vivekananda. In him everything is positive and nothing negative." Vivekananda realized a country's future depends on its people, so he mainly stressed on man, "man-making is my mission", that is how he described his teaching. Vivekananda put his real ideals in few words and that was: "to preach unto mankind their divinity, and how to make it manifest in every movement of life". For over twelve years from 1890-1902, amidst much hardship, suffering and personal humiliation, Swami Vivekananda toured all over India and to several places abroad as itinerant monk, preaching and working on diverse problems. He played a major role in introducing India and her spiritual culture of Vedānta to the Western world and in reviving and refining Hinduism within India. His main teachings may be summarized in terms of his views on education, religion. character building, womanhood, Hinduism, spirit of service and national integration. A unique feature of Vivekananda's teachings is that they are, by and large, of universal nature, and hence, his speeches and sayings have been quoted by Albert Einstein, Nikola Tesla, Jawaharlal Nehru and many others.

## NOTES

1. *Complete Works of Swami Vivekananda*, Vol. 1, p. 124.
2. *Ibid.*, Vol. 13, p. 302.
3. *Guru Bani of Kabir.*
4. *Śrīmadbhāgavata Mahāpurāṇa.*
5. *Complete Works of Swami Vivekananda*, Vol. 1, p. 358.
6. *Ibid.*, Vol. 1, 10th edition, p. 28.
7. *Education*, Swami Vivekananda, p. 4.
8. *Prabuddha Bharata*, A monthly Journal of Sri Ramakrishna Order. January 2000.

# 14

# Education and Globalization

## A Philosophical Study

*Kumkum Sinha*

Globalization is essentially a process of dramatic and drastic reduction of distances and isolation by electronic media and other powerful means of communication. This indeed is a new phenomenon, but the process of unification of people coming together, of ideas merging with one another, has been going on from time immemorial. Says Swami Vivekananda:

> "Two forces seem to be working throughout nature. One of these is constantly differentiating and the other is constantly unifying: the one making more and more for separate individuals, the other, as it were, bringing the individual into a mass, bringing out sameness in the midst of all this differentiation. ..."[1]
>
> "...The idea of oneness has had its advocates throughout all times. From the days of Upaniṣads, the Buddhas, and Christs, and all other great preachers of religion, down to our present day, in the new political aspirations, and in the claims of

> the oppressed and the downtrodden ... comes out the one assertion of this unity and sameness."[2]

The buzzword today is "globalization", whose essence is the unity of everything: seeking and finding the universe in this apparent multiverse. The appeal of the Upaniṣads today is that they contain the only philosophy by which the whole universe can be united, globalized. In fact, Vedānta, the philosophy of the Upaniṣads says that one cannot even talk of globalization, for it would mean that we are trying make global something which was not global already. In "globalize", we have the suffix, "ize", the *abhuta-tadbhāva, chvi pratyaya* of Sanskrit grammer, which means that something was not global earlier, and we are now making it so.

Globalization is a process, which has affected many areas of human life, one of those being education. In the twentieth century. Many developing countries have experienced growth in the educational facilities available to them due to the entry of institutions from the West. Some believe that this process is an invaluable opportunity for the people of the developing countries to raise their skills and standards of education. Others fear that it is merely a modern version of cultural imperialism that will lead to the creation of a universal, ultimately Western society. One aspect of the globalization of education has been the creation of "twinning projects" between one Western and one non-Western university). Through Globalization of education, which is being knowledge transfer from the Western countries into developing countries, is intended to improve the skills and capabilities of the people receiving it.

The great philosopher Socrates had said "Education is not the filling of a vessel, but the kindling of a flame."[3] The word "education" itself comes from the word *educere*, which means to bring out what is already in and not blindly stuff in. The purpose of education is to detect talent proactively. For this, it is essential that education has to be based on application and intelligence (with open book exams wherever necessary) instead of trying to test memory of knowledge. This is especially so in the era of Internet where everybody can have the knowledge, but it is only one's intelligence with which one can distinguish or differentiate oneself. Memory does not have that much significance since everything is there on the net—its application that should matter and be tested. Since people tend to remember more of what they happen to be interested in, memory can be a tool to know vocation instead of an end in itself. Children can be made aware of main memory techniques.

Einstein had said that "Imagaination is more important than knowledge"[4]. Each person's imagaination is diffferent and therefore, he has to be guided correctly to chose his occupation in life where he is going to spend a majority of waking hours. Not doing so would be disastrous as pointed out by so many of our spiritual staly stalwarts. Swami Vivekananda said, "Education is the manifestation of perfection already present in man"[5]—Unless there is perfection in education, that perfection cannot be drawn out. Real education should enable you to find out what is uniquely you. That is what matters in practical life, not bookish knowledge.

In our culture today, there is a huge emphasis on education, especially higher education. Society basically says the more educated you are, the better off you are. That is pretty much true if you live by the means of society. The basic idea that education, especially a college education, is something that people should pursue even into their adult years is not by any means a new idea.

Every society has specialized individuals who fulfil certain positions that require extended education. In some cases, these people are known as shamans, priests, or professors, or they may be doctors, mechanics, blacksmiths, or artists. In all these professions, some form of higher education is necessary. It could come from an apprentice or rigorous private study, or it could take the form of a formal higher education. Whatever the form, the meaning is the same, gain knowledge and use it.

The idea of education has been a big part of each and every culture on earth. However, as we all know, there are many questions on what it means to be educated.

In ancient times, the total education was concentrated on the establishment of the existence of God, heaven and hell. If justice is followed, God rewards you with heaven and if injustice is done, God punishes you in the hell. If you say that God exists. People may not believe and may commit sins by which the balance of the society gets disturbed. The existence of God is to be proved through very deep logical analysis and discussions. All the seminars and conferences in ancient India ran on single subject, which is about the existence and nature of God. Today, people think that the ancient scholars in India wasted lot of time on this useless subject. Today, scholars spend lot of time on seminars and debates dealing with developments of new materials. Machines and applications of energy. In fact, the ancient scholars were highly wise and the modern scholars are highly foolish.

The results of the present research in science are leading to the improvement of several amenities of the humanity. But, these amenities are now realized to be the ways of destruction of the environment leading to global calamity in a very short period of time. Our ancient scholars did not encourage such research in science since the advanced knowledge of energy and materials will lead to the destruction of humanity. Moreover, they concentrated on the logical understanding of the existence of God so that the resulting balanced society without corruption and chaos will give immense happiness to the life of the humanity. We now realize that the ancient materials and technologies were far better for health and environmental balance of the world. Added to this happiness, a strong fear for God and hell were well established in the mind of every human being through long period of spiritual education.

Little knowledge of materials and technologies was sufficient for the happiness of humanity and to maintain the ecological balance. This aspect is at the external physical level. Regarding the internal intellectual level, intensified realization resulted in every human being regarding the existence of God. After a long period of learning, the human being came out of the ancient university with thorough realization of the existence of God, hell and heaven so that in the practical life, the human being perfectly followed the justice rejecting the injustice at any cost. People did not know even the word "corruption" because everybody was afraid of God and hell. Today, after a long period of learning. The person coming out of the modern university is not at all in touch with the subject of God. Moreover, the person is well versed in the technologies of energy and materials and is dedicating the total life for increasing amenities, which ultimately lead to environmental pollution and global destruction.

The present human being is well versed in the concepts of profit and loss and is a master of business administration. Everybody wants to improve the personal amenities even through corruption. Corruption has become a spontaneous global phenomenon. Metals undergo corrosion and the human beings undergo the process of corruption. The government has become corrupt. The government officials are corrupt. Even the judiciary system has become corrupt. In such atmosphere of powerful corruption and corrupt human beings, can you expect a system like *lokapāla* to work perfectly to control the corruption? When all the human beings are corrupt, the members of the *lokapāla* also become corrupt. You cannot bring the angels from heaven to appoint them as members of *lokapāla*. After sometime, you will have to bring another control in the system to control the *lokapāla*s! There will be no end to this and the desired aim can never be fulfilled.

The only solution for this is to revert back to the ancient system and concentrate on spiritual education. Today, the government does not spend a single rupee on the propagation of spiritual education. Only a few persons in private and personal sector like saints are taking interest in propagating the spiritual education. At least, the huge funds of very important temples like Tirupati should be spent on the propagation of spiritual education. You are starting colleges and universities with the funds of such temple, in which again the materialistic education is propagated. Kings used to construct huge temples and spend lot of money on temples. In fact, these temples were the universities in which learned professors of the spiritual education propagated the spiritual knowledge in the humanity. Lot of encouragement was given by kings to this spiritual knowledge, which controls crime and corruption from the basic level itself. Even if you spend 1/10th of what you spend on the control of crime and corruption for the sake of the propagation of spiritual knowledge, the crime and corruption will disappear from the root itself.

The government should open its eyes on this basic issue and reform the education system in the light of this concept. The negligence of the present blind government on spiritual education is the main reason for the present crime and corruption in the society. The present system of education stressing mainly on science and technology for improving the amenities of humanity is the reason for the environmental pollution and the future untimely global destruction. If you revert back to the ancient education system, every human being will come out as a citizen with in-built aversion to corruption and crime. Such ancient education, concentrated on God, will also reduce the over attachment to amenities and this will lead to ecological balance and global safety.

For the sake of control of crime and corruption, the existence of God need not be accepted. Such acceptance will be based on falsehood and such realization is not real. Moreover, the result of such false realization will not be true also. It means that the control of crime and corruption cannot be achieved by forcing you to accept the existence of God for the sake of control of corruption and crime. The realization of existence of God should be independent and should not be for any purpose. Whether the crime and corruption are controlled or not, the existence of God should be realized on its own merit and truth. What I mean to say is that the ancient scholars did not create the concept of God for the sake of control of crime and corruption to achieve the balance of society. The existence of God was realized as the independent concept on the credit of its own merit.

The ancient education system was composed of several schools like logic (Tarka), grammar (Vyākaraṇa), analysis of sacred scriptures (Mīmāṁsā), etc. and all the schools aimed at the subject of God (philosophy) only. The student, after realizing the existence of God with the help of all the schools of education (Śāstras), comes out as a citizen fearing for crime and corruption. Therefore, the existence of God is primary basis and the control of corruption and crime is the secondary consequence. Hence, it is wrong, as some people say, that the concept of God by itself is not true, but, should be respected and maintained for the sake of control of crime and corruption. In such a way, the crime and corruption can never be controlled because one knows that the basic concept is only created story for control in crime and corruption.

Natural talent often manifests well without any formal coaching. I played lawn Tennis for several years but was not satisfied with the backhand (bane of many racquet games). My younger brother got it right in the first week itself without any coaching in such a brilliant manner that many players complimented him. My wife is qualified in English hons but it is me, an MBA who has written articles and poems for magazines and newspapers. Similarly, she does certain business work much better than I do. My father does much better trading in shares than me despite not having any formal training in technical analysis (graphs) which I have. I once worked in a company where the rise of one person was much faster than four others though all of them were from the same batch from the same institute. Talent is more important than the tool (knowledge).

Education must also impart good vocational and physical training and inculcate values to respect all vocations/ professions—that is something we have to learn from the United States where a janitor can talk to a professor on one to one basis on the same table as an equal. The caste system which determines occupations by birth is fundamentally incorrect. All that also causes inter-personal problems in practical management.

In books like *Karma, Destiny and Career*, it is given what can happen if you try to pursue an exalted occupation (lawyer, doctor) when in reality your real vocation maybe relatively humble (carpenter, plumber). In New York, a child psychologist became a taxi driver because driving was his passion. (This may seem absurd, but normally people seeking artistic satisfaction have such problems.) Therefore, formal education should give equal respect to all occupations and people should be respected for what they are instead of snobishness of degrees and qualifications associated with certain exalted professions.

There is a difference between being wise, being knowledgeable, being well informed and being intelligent—such disctinction should be clearly made to the students so that some of their false and baseless fears subside and there is a reduction in the number of board exam suicides which have gone up considerably in the past five years. Students should also be trained to be wary of "Information pollution" since they confuse being knowledgeable with intelligence which is why this is such a relevant question.

Practical knowledge is best—Osho specified that there is a difference between knowledge (bookish) and knowing (experience). With role plays and group dynamics, the latter can be imparted in some disciplines and not left to the vagaries of practical experience. The twenty-first century is expected to be stressful and therefore *yoga* and meditation should also be taught properly in schools. Physical fitness was stressed by Swami Vivekananda and we have a lot to learn from the Western world just the way they learn *yoga* from us. Unfortunately, education has become a business and nobody is bothered about the real purpose of education and one ends up paying more in donation and not getting any real education. It's a loss both ways like "Heads I win, Tails you lose". Whether, it is education or anything else, unless there is a continuous and consistent monitoring mechanism, nobody shall be accountable and nothing shall have lasting success.

> "Mahatma Gandhi, the father of the nation gave the scheme of education for modern India, which can be called the first blue print of national system of education, which is job centred, value based and mass oriented. It is the first model of vocationalization of education in India. In Gandhi an scheme of education, knowledge must be related to activity and practical experience. His scheme of education envisages, a close integration between the schools and community so as to make child more social minded and cooperative. Need of the hour is to reorient education so as to channelize the manpower in the right direction. In the reports of the various committees and commissions the need and the importance of education has been emphasized to make it vocational, i.e. job oriented and productive for self-employment. With the serious problem of mounting educated unemployed young men and women, growing unrest among the students, re-orientation of the educational system on the spirit of Gandhian

conception of education seems to be the need of the twenty-first century."[6]

In Jaina ideology, we get indication of two kinds of education: (1) *Grahana śikṣā*—Theoretical knowledge, and (2) *Āsevaṇa śikṣā*—Practical knowledge. The former is the knowledge gained from the *guru* or a teacher or a treatise, while the later is the applied knowledge gained by putting into practice the former one. Although, in today's scientific field, the second type of education is going on, yet the practical training for bringing about these desired transformation in the consciousness (at mental and emotional levels) is lacking even there. For the development of the values promoting good conduct and behaviour. It is necessary to regulate/balance the *cetanā* (consciousness), especially at subconscious or unconscious level. To fulfil this we have developed a system of "Science of Living" under the auspices of Late Ācārya Śrī Tulsī, the founder of the Aṇuvrata. The Yogic postures (*yogāsana*), breathing exercise (*prāṇāyāma*), perceptive meditation (*prekṣā dhyāna*), relaxation exercise (*kāyotsarga*) together with self-awareness, auto-suggestion and contemplation (*bhāvanā, aṇuprekṣa*) comprise the strategy of the science of living; the practical exercises of all these are to be done for the transformation of consciousness. This practice is useful for the students of science as for those of the arts faculty.

In the Pāli literature of Prākṛt languages, we get a beautiful education—"Education ought to achieve two objects—(1) To solve the problem of livelihood. (2) To attain *sadgati*, i.e. to develop the values of life or values promoting good conduct." In the absence of the above-said values, it is not possible to awaken the "good" in human nature, to construct a healthy society.

Education has a great social importance especially in the modern, complex industrialized societies. Philosophers of all periods, beginning with ancient stages, devoted to it a great deal of attention. Accordingly, various theories regarding its nature and objective have come into being. Let us now examine some of the significant functions of education.

## 1. To Complete the Socialization Process

The main social objective of education is to complete the socialization process. The family gets the child, but the modern family tends to leave much undone in the socialization process. The school and other institutions have come into being in place of family to complete the socialization process. Now, the people fell that it is "the school's business to train the whole child even to the extent of teaching him honesty, fair play, consideration for others and a sense of right and wrong". The school devotes much, of its time and energy to the matter such as cooperation, good citizenship, doing one's duty and upholding the law. Directly through textbooks and indirectly through celebration of programmes patriotic sentiments are intimates and instilled. The nation's past is glorified, its legendary heroes respected, and its military ventures justified.

## 2. To Transmit the Central Heritage

All societies maintain themselves, by exploitation of a culture. Culture here refers to a set of beliefs and skills, art, literature, philosophy, religion, music, etc. that are not carried through the mechanism of heredity. They must be learned. This social heritage (culture) must be transmitted through social organizations. Education has this function of cultural transmission in all societies. It is only at the under leaves of the school that any serious attempt has been, or now is, made to deal with this area.

## 3. For the Formation of Social Personality

Individual must have personalities shaped or fashioned in

ways that fit into the culture. Education everywhere has the function of the formation of social personalities. Education helps in transmitting culture through proper molding of social personalities. In this way, it contributes to the integration, to survive and to reproduce themselves.

## 4. Reformation of Attitudes

Education aims at the reformation of attitudes wrongly developed by children already. For various reasons the child may have absorbed a host of attitudes, beliefs and disbeliefs, loyalties, and prejudices, jealously and hatred, etc. these are to be reformed. It is the function of education to see that unfounded beliefs, illogical prejudices and unreasoned loyalties are removed from the child's mind, though the school has its own limitations in this regard, it is expected to continue its efforts in reforming the attitudes of the child.

## 5. Education for Occupational Placement

An instrument of livelihood. Education has a practical and also it should help the adolescent for earning his livelihood. Education has come to be today as nothing more than an instrument of livelihood. It should enable the student to take out his livelihood. Education must prepare the student for future occupational positions, the youth should be enabled to play a productive role in society. Accordingly, great emphasis has been placed on vocational training.

## 6. Conferring of Status

Conferring of status is one of the most important functions of education. The amount of education one has, is correlated with his class position. This is four in USA, USSR, Japan, Germany and some other societies. Education is related to one's position in the stratification structure in two ways: (1) An evaluation of one's status is partially decided by what kind of education one has received; and (2) Many of the other important criteria of class position such as occupation, income and style of life are partially the result of the type and amount of education one has had. Men who finish college, for example, earn two and a half times as much as those who have a grammar school education.

## 7. Education Encourages the Spirit of Competition

The school instills cooperative values through civic and patriotic exhortation or advice. Yet, the school's main emphasis is upon personal competition. For each subject studied the child is compared with the companies by percentage of marks or rankings. The teacher admires and praises those who do well and frowns upon those who fail to do well. The school's ranking system serves to prepare for a later ranking system. Many of those who are emotionally disappointed by low ranking in the school are thereby prepared to accept limited achievement in the larger world outside the school.

### *Other Functions of Education*

Peter Worsley has spoken of a few more functions of education. Some of them may be noted, Education Trains in skills that are required by the economy. The relation between the economy and education can be an exact one. For example, the number and productive capacity of engineering firms are limited by the number of engineers produced by education. In planned economy, normally it is planned years in advance to produce a definite number of doctors, engineers, teachers, technicians, scientists, etc. to meet the social and economic needs of the society.

### *Fosters Participant Democracy*

Education fosters participant democracy. Participant

democracy in any large and complex society depends on literacy. Literacy allows full participation of the people in democratic processes and effective voting. Literacy is a product of education. Educational system has this economic as well as political significance.

### *Education Imparts Values*

The curriculum of the school, its extracurricular activities and the informal relationships amongst students and teacher communicate social skills and values. Through various activities a school imparts values such as cooperation or atmospheric, audience, fair play. Thin is also done through curriculum that is through lessons in history, literature, etc.

## Education Acts as an Integrative Force

Education acts as integrative force in society by communicating value that unite different sections of society. The family may fail to provide the child the essential knowledge of the social skills and value of the wider society. The school or the educational institutions can help the child to learn new skills and learn to interact with people of different social backgrounds.

### *Values and Orientations, which are Specific to Certain Occupations, are also Provided by Education*

For example, the medical students are socialized and educated in a particular way in medical college. This may help them to become proper medical practitioners, other values and orientations relevant to the functioning of industrial society are also provided by education.

The principal objective of education has been the development of the whole individual. The minimum level of education that was necessary to achieve this goal in the agrarian society was basic or primary and in the industrial age, secondary. In the present borderless information society, education needs to be able to respond to additional demands of a rapidly globalizing world by raising awareness of environment, peace, cultural, and social diversity, increased competitiveness, and the concept of a global village. Such education is to a knowledge or information society what secondary education was to an industrial economy. Education prepares the individual to connect—and live in harmony—with the environment around him. Globalization has changed the size, nature, and quality of that environment. The challenge for higher education, therefore, is to reform, create and develop systems that prepare the individual to work in a borderless economy and live in a global society. In other words, our educational institutions need to produce global citizens.

One of the major consequences of the globalization of education has been commodification and the corporatization of institutions of higher learning. It is said that the for-profit education market in the United States is worth more than $500 billion in revenue for the involved corporates. More than one thousand state schools have been handed over to corporations to be run as businesses. But there is a fundamental problem with the way business models have been applied to the delivery of education and other public goods. Unthinking adoption of the private sector model prevents the development of a meaningful approach to management in the public services in general or to the social services in particular based on their distinctive purposes, conditions and objectives.

There is another, more serious, problem with corporatization of education. Corporations operate on the principles of cost reduction and profit maximization. These require introducing standardization and the packaging of product in compact, measurable, byte-like, configuration. Applied to education, these approaches would possibly negate its basic fabric and purpose. Education has always encouraged and represents openness, inquiry, diversity, research, and limitless learning. Corporatization of education would make it elitist—the one provided by corporations for the masses and the poor who cannot afford going to the traditional institutions of learning, and the other for the rich and the affluent.

Thus, our present educational system is producing a quality of life that suffers from depression and psychiatric disorders flowering from the deterioration in our social environment. There has been an increasing rise in violent crimes, terrorism, accidents, suicides, sexually transmitted diseases, alcoholism, and drug abuse. Whether we talk about cancer or crime figures, inflation or unemployment, traffic jams or energy shortages, the dynamic underlying these problems is the same. There are systematic problems, which means that they are closely interconnected and interdependent, and are partly the outcome of our specialized system of education which is bereft of cultural and spiritual value.

The principal objective of education has been the development of the whole individual. The minimum level of education that was necessary to achieve this goal in the agrarian society was basic or primary and in the industrial age, secondary. In the present borderless information society, education needs to be able to respond to additional demands of a rapidly globalizing world by raising awareness of environment, peace, cultural and social diversity, increased competitiveness, and the concept of a global village. Such education is to a knowledge or information society what secondary education was to an industrial economy. Education prepares the individual to connect—and live in harmony with the environment around him. Globalization has changed the size, nature and quality of that environment. The challenge for higher education, therefore, is to reform, create and develop systems that prepare the individual to work in a borderless economy and live in a global society. In other words, our educational institutions need to produce global citizens.

## NOTES

1. *Complete Works of Swami Vivekananda*, Vol. 1, p. 430.
2. *Ibid.*, Vol. 1, p. 431.
3. Socrates, *Greek Philosophy*, p. 12.
4. *Einstein*.
5. *Complete Works of Swami Vivekananda*, Vol. 1, p. 81.
6. *The Indian Journal of Political Science* (2005). Indian Political Science Association.
7. Late Ācārya Śrī Tulsī, the founder of the Aṇuvrata.

# 15

# Education, Ethics and Values

*Rajjan Kumar* and *Sunita Kumari*

Education in Hindi language *śikṣā* is a process of acquisition and transmission of knowledge. Education is a preparation of life and man-making. Thus, education has aims, objectives and purposes and itself has own value. Why "ethics of education" or "ethics in education" or "value of education" or "value in education"? Ethics deal with right and norms. Ethics is a system or code of morals. Values do not mean only virtues. Moral values are known as virtues. Once someone knows his values and knows what is important to him, ethics can help him to set goals. "Ethics of education" or "ethics in education" or "value of education" or "value in education" can be understood by referring a quotation of Swami Vivekananda as he said,

> "the ideal of all education, all training should be man-making. Education is not the amount of information that is put into your brain and runs riot there, undigested, all your life. We must have life-building, man-making and character-making assimilation of ideas."

Education is a continuous process of acquisition and transmission of knowledge. Education should be ethical, moral and value oriented. Before undertaking the exposition of ethics in education it will be helpful to first explain the meaning and nature of ethical and value-orientation in education as it is the essence of education itself. It should be remembered that the quest after ethics and values and the attainment of values constitute the very core of human existence. There is an innate necessity in a human being to participate in the process of ethical and value realization. This is caused by his/her imperfection and finitude and awareness thereof. That is why, consciously or unconsciously ethics, morality, value-concepts, value-discriminations, and value-judgements feature prominently in his/her life. Let us also not forget that the process of ethical consciousness and value realization is basically educational and it tends to refer to set of morality and values embodied and expressed in the objectives for which education is imparted.

Since education must have some definite objectives if it has to be meaningful, effective and of any worth, it is quite natural to ask, "What is it that education thrives to accomplish?" A consideration of this question necessitates a sort of ethical and value-thinking, for it is ethical and value-decisions alone which can provide valid and adequate objectives. Ethics and value considerations are so widely pervading the sphere of education that all educational decisions presuppose or involve moral and value-decisions. For examples, what is to be taught (ends and objectives involved in the curricula), how is to be taught (methods), whom is it be taught (fitness, motivation, and interest of the student), how to evaluate the performance of the students, etc. are the issues which demand ethical and value considerations. In all educational activities ethical and value-involvement is inevitable.

Once we have grasped the fact the nature of human being and therefore of education are such as to require him/her to participate in the fullness of life, to be receptive of the significant and to be open to whatever has meaning and value, the question arises as to what is valuable in life and in the world. In other words, what should we appreciate and imbibe so as to be a person in the full sense of the term. The question in short is how we can discern the values of human life and existence. In order to get right answer, it may be profitable to look at the various thought in this regard.

According to the Vedas education is the basic means to attain perfection and freedom. And there is no other way. A real education is that which helps us in realizing this state (*sa vidyā yā vimuktaye*). So, the ultimate goal of Vedic education is man-making. It should turn out a *puruṣa* a genuine human being (*manurbhava janaya daivyam—Ṛgveda* X.53.63). From this goal all aims and objectives of education should follow as corollaries. A true education must help in enabling us to live a quality life, a life which is worth living, through a balanced, harmonious, and all round development of the individual, the society and the entire cosmos. This is what meant by ethical and value-oriented education, both in the sense of ethics of education, or ethics in education and values in education or values of education.

Education is a preparation of life. But life is not mere livelihood. Similarly life is not mere catering to demands of matter or spirit, body or soul. There is no exclusive either or between them. No human being is merely a professional being whether an ordinary worker or a scantiest or an engineer of a doctor or an industrialist, etc. likewise no human being is a recluse or *saṁnyāsī*. The Vedic thought adopts a holistic approach to life and reality and therefore calls for the education of the whole human being and not just get confirmed to some aspects only. Hence, the fullness of education consists in and must comprise all the facets of existence—physical, vital, mental, intellectual, and spiritual.

In the *Taittirīya Upaniṣad*, we have an illuminating account of these five dimensions of human personality. It is known as the theory of *pañcakośa* (Bhṛguvallī I.6). In their togetherness they constitute the total personality. Following the Vedic view in the modern times Swami Vivekananda, Sri Aurobindo, Rabindranath Tagore, Mahatma Gandhi, etc. have emphasized that a true and adequate education must aim at the total person. It can be argued that the above account and analysis may be theoretically sound, but the question is how to put it into practice. Its practical viability can be demonstrated by providing a blueprint of the education for the values of matter.

A thing of value is a joy forever. Anything with the quality of *sat*, *cit* and *ānanda* is in itself a thing of value. It is value that satisfies the feeling of worthwhileness. However, it is so complex that it defies all attempts at definitions. Different approaches to axiology bring about the idealist, the naturalist, the realist, the pragmatist, the reconstructienists, the existentialist and even the transcendentalist views of values. However, what goes often unnoticed is the fact the "knowledge" itself is value, and by extension "education" is also a value. Which kind of value education itself has. To support this we quote a verse from the *Mahābhārata, śīla-vṛtta-phalam śrutam,* i.e. character and conduct is the fruits of learning. But how does one impart such education? The Mother has said:

> "It is above all through example—that education becomes effective. To speak good words and to give wise advice to a child has very little effect if one does not oneself give him an example of what one teaches. Sincerity, honesty, straightforwardness, courage, disinterestedness, unselfishness, patience, endurance, perseverance, peace, calm, self-control are all things that are taught infinitely better by example than by beautiful speeches."

In our Śāstras the information-based knowledge is called *apara-vidyā* while the state in which the intellect becomes quite, it is *para-vidyā*. In this state there is no ego, no centre.

There is no process of becoming. There is only the state of being. There is unity of life, no feeling of otherness, no fear. In this state of consciousness, there will not be conflict, violence, exploitation, and war. At mental level all these are present. But when man goes above mind, in the superconscious, the dimension gets changed. Now action does not come from ego, but from intelligence, unity of life, totality of life. Insanity and animality of mind are washed away and society becomes saner. In education one must teach about this dimension of the mind as also about the way how to reach that state. Swami Vivekananda named it as divinity. He preached that manifestation of divinity in man is the real purpose of education.

Right from the beginning the purpose of education has been confronted with two terms named *preyas* and *śreyas*, i.e. pleasant and good, materialism and spiritualism as the twin objectives of life as well as education. Both are as old as man on the earth. *Preyas* is ingrained in all human beings. It signifies all worldly desires including food and sex. Man is usually engaged in solving the problems of life, in acquisition of food, wealth, name, fame, and physical enjoyment. The physical world appears most real to him as it is most familiar. But man is a rational animal. Spirituality or *śreyas* being the expression of man's rationality also originated with man and consequently it developed along with man's intellectual progress. The balanced blending of these two—*preyas* and *śreyas*—makes a man a perfect human being. Likewise education does. The basic role of education is to attain perfection and man making.

The aim of education is twofold: collective and individual. At the collective level, the aim is to make an individual into a good citizen; i.e., a person with harmonious relationship with other members of the community, a person useful to the society and one who fulfils his obligations as a citizen. At the individual level the student expects an educational institution to help him develop a strong and healthy body, build his character attain self-mastery and supply him opportunities to discover and realize his natural abilities.

Both expectations are justified, but it is necessary to understand the relationship between the individual and society and that aspirations of the two needs to be mutually harmonized. The human mind tends to emphasize one or the other and the current dominant thought is that individual interest must be subordinated to societal interest. Therefore, the collective aim of education, ethics, and values has overshadowed the individual aim and the chief challenge facing educators is how to fit the individual to the demands of the society.

Apart from this kind of thought we must observe a fact that any system of education, in order to be effective in promoting peace and happiness, must be based on the structure, growth, and working of the human mind. At the same time, its foundations must be firmly rooted in ethnic culture, heritage, and socio-economic environment. Reflecting the basic concepts of Indian philosophy in his views on education, ethics, and values, Swami Vivekananda observed, "Education is the manifestation of perfection already in man". Education policies must be framed taking into account the infinite and perfect knowledge is in everyone waiting to be discovered and unveiled through personal effort and with the help and guidance of those who have had some experience of revelation of knowledge within.

When somebody asked Gandhiji, "What is your goal in education?" Gandhiji replied, "Character building. I would try to develop courage, strength, virtue, the ability to forget oneself in working towards great aim. This is more important than literacy, academic learning is only a means to this greater end." Literacy is neither the beginning, nor the end of education, "Literary training by itself adds not an inch to one's moral height and character-building is independent of literary training." Here, we remember the words of Albert Einstein according to whom,

> "the most important human endeavour is the striving for morality in our actions. Our inner balance and even our very existence depend on it. Only morality in our actions can give beauty and dignity to life."

This helps us to assimilate or explain the relationship among ethics, values, and education.

To define the aims, objectives and ideals of education one observes that it is ethical and having values which helps people to serve human world in many ways. Rusk very much said, "The aim of education is the enhancement of personality, the differentiating feature of which the embodiment of universal values." Further he quotes,

> "Education must be enable mankind through its culture to enter more and more fully into the spiritual realm and also to enlarge the boundaries of the spiritual realm."

Frobel extend the ethical and moral ideals of education to explain the objective of education as,

> "The object of education is the realization of a faithful, pure inviolate and hence holy life. Education should lead and guide man to clearness concerning him and in himself, to face with Nature and to unity with God".

Ethics and value in education must be recognized by quoting Plato, "Education consists of giving the body and the soul all perfection of which they are susceptible". Further he said

> "I mean by education that training which is given by suitable habits to the first instinct of virtue in

> children ... which leads you always to hate what you ought to hate and love what you ought to love, from the beginning of life to the end ... in my view will be rightly called education."

This view of ethics of education has been supported and elaborated by John Dewey to consider education as social efficiency, cultivation of power and sharing as common activities. All education proceeds by the participation of the individual in the social consciousness of the race. Education is a continuous process of adjustment having its aim at every stage an added capacity of growth.

Apart from the religion preachers and spiritualists, educators, philosophers, social reformers, sociologists, and thinkers have reflected upon the meaning and dimensions of the concept ethics, value, and education. Although their views differ widely, but all of them stress the significance of values, ethics and education in terms of "values" at personal, national, and global level. In view of the divergence of opinion on the concept, the noted philosopher A.C. Garnet in *Religion and Moral Life* (1955) observed that on account of the ambiguity of the term "value", it should be avoided except where the contextual meaning is clear.

In terms of "ethics of education" words like values, virtues, morality along with ethics are used. To clarify all those we present some lines from the write-up of B. Mukhopadhyaya published in *University News* (7-13 March 2005) has attempted to differentiate value-related terms. He has observed,

> "... Values do not mean only virtues. Moral values are known as virtues. Ethics deal with right and norms. Ethics is a system or code of morals. Once someone knows his values and knows what is important to him, ethics can help him to set goals."

Values involve individual feelings, ideas and beliefs an individual operates according to a system of values. Everything he does, every decision he makes, comes from within, conscious or unconscious system of value. The Committee on Moral Education, Uttar Pradesh (1983), considers moral education and value-oriented education as one and the same thing. It, in its report on moral education, has given a wider meaning to it. It has interpreted it "to include not only ethical values, but also spiritual, scientific, aesthetic, and sporting values, indeed all humanistic values". More vividly the phrase "value education" is preferred to other terms in vogue like "moral education", "value education", "moral and spiritual education", etc., in view of its comprehensiveness, the concern is with the development of values in general that covers moral, social, spiritual, aesthetic, and other values as well [*Education in Values: A Source Book*, published by NCERT, 1992].

The National Policy of Education (1986) highlights the urgent need for value education in view of growing erosion of essential values and increasing cynicism in society. With a well-designed system of curriculum, it is possible to make education a forceful tool for the cultivation desirable ethical, moral, spiritual, and social values. Education should foster universal and eternal values. Value education should help to eliminate obscurantism, religious fanatism, violence, superstition, and fatalism. Education which inculcates universal and eternal values like compassion, courage, honesty, tolerance, and truthfulness, etc., will help in developing balanced individuals and in creating a humane society.

A value stands for ideals men live for. Values are part and parcel of the philosophy of a nation and that of its educational system. They are guiding principles of life which are conducive to all round development. The philosophy of values is described by Vivekananda in these words,

> "To be happy is the universal urge of all beings and at all times. One has to be at peace with oneself to be happy. These can be no peace for a turbulent mind. *Vāsanā*s (undesirable, wants) take away

> peace of mind. It is only when we follow a value system that we can have a serene, contemplative mind. When mind is calm, we can turn it within to 'see' the treasure of pure consciousness. No treasure, on earth is equal to a slice of that *tattva* (element)."

Values form an important element of the personality of individuals which influences their thought and behaviour in an unconscious manner. They are normative standards by which human beings are influenced in the choice among alternative courses of action. It is, therefore, very essential that education should develop such values in the students that they become an asset and guide them to become individuals of sterling character who place service of the society above service of the self. Importance of value in education can be distinguished as *Śrīmad Bhagavadgītā* states, "Mind, has to be loosened from *dūrtyapara* (misleads) and engaged in acquiring *sadguṇa* (virtues). A mind which has *daivī sampatti* (divine qualities) has *śānti* (peace)." These values make us introspective and correct our personality. Values are various kinds and named according to their specifications:

- Aesthetic values in accordance with arts, dancing, painting, dramatization, music, etc.
- Spiritual values concerning spirit as opposed to matter.
- Moral values relating to ethics.
- Social values concerning society.

Apart from the above classification values can be considered as: instrumental values, intrinsic values, cultural values, essential values, personal values, social values, national values, global values, ethical values, and spiritual values. These are not a rigid classification of values. All values overlap to some degree.

## REFERENCES

Agrawal, J.C. (2005). *Education for Values, Environment and Human Rights*. Delhi: Shipra Publications.

Chattopadhyaya, D.P. (Ed. 2000). *Quest for Excellence.* New Delhi: Richa Prakashan.

Joshi, Kireet (Ed. 2002). *Philosophy of Value-Oriented Education Theory & Practice*. New Delhi: Indian Council of Philosophical Research.

# 16

# Buddhist Ethics and Education

*D.C. Srivastava*

In the mainstream of the West, education is viewed simply as gaining knowledge, skills, or other forms of human capital that will assist one in earning a living sufficient to buy human security. This perspective will not get us very far—although, it is a truism that everyone has the right to an education and training. But the matter does not simply rest there. What kind of education are we talking about? Is literacy merely measured by the ability to read and write? To be able to see an atrocity as an atrocity and to realize less violent futures may require something radically different from the education presently offered in the mainstream.

An alternative perspective has been put forward by some creative Western minds. Adam Curle, fore instance, has suggested that "Education is a learning process that pulls out the hidden potentials in each person, that facilitates self-creation through self-realization."

Similarly, a fundamental objective of Buddhist education is to pull out the hidden potentials in each person so that each individual might realize his or her full potential, or what is often referred to as Buddha nature. Buddha nature is something that cannot be realized automatically. Rather, it requires collective action or social engagement. And perhaps most important, it requires non-violence. Non-violence may be considered as the master precept of Buddhism. As such, a proper Buddhist education would foster a culture of peace, which entails, among others, subduing the rising tide of human insecurity, structural violence, and terror through compassion, humility, generosity, mindfulness and wisdom.

## Buddhist Education and Value

We are all familiar with the story of Prince Siddhārtha. For the first third of his life, Prince Siddhārtha was confined to a life of luxury by a concerned but overly-protective father. A complicated system of blinders and misinformation made it all, but impossible for the Prince to gain a proper perspective of the world. But, curiosity eventually pushed the young Prince beyond the faśade and into the streets of his kingdom. While walking amongst the commoners he saw four things which transformed him: a sick person, an old man, a corpse, and a wandering ascetic. Upon experiencing the reality of existence the Buddha became quite inquisitive and sought to abandon his lifestyle in a noble attempt to understand and ultimately eliminate suffering.

From this story, we can see that Buddhist pedagogy does not separate life from education. To do so is to run the risk of misunderstanding the world. Increasingly, in living, one is always on the move, encountering new people and experiences. The process of understanding life therefore cannot be realized by rejecting the world, but by working for social justice and change. Buddhists are thus recommended to confront *dukkha* or suffering not to hide from it and, equally important, to contemplate on its causes, which are linked directly or indirectly with greed (*lobha*) and/or lust (*rāga*), hatred (*doṣa*), and delusion (*moha*) or ignorance (*avidyā*). All these root causes of evil, Buddhist would argue, could be eradicated, if we educate ourselves properly in morality (*śīla*), mindfulness (*samādhi*) and understanding or wisdom (*paññā*).

The Nobel Laureate Amartya Sen suggested once in a Human Security Conference that Prince Siddhārtha's story is one of the first recorded instances of humanity's interest in human security. Like the young Prince Siddhārtha, we should try to understand how the suffering we experience is linked to our view or assumptions of the universe and consequently how our invented social structures and economic systems perpetuate our pain. This opens up space for cognitive diversity, for different forms of knowledge, which may be equally valid. For instance, certain forms of knowledge are needed to get men to the moon, while others are needed to foster environmental sustainability. Certain forms of knowledge are needed to build super-bombs, but certain forms of knowledge are needed to make peace. This is sheer common sense, and lots of examples may be drawn from daily life. If modern medicine cannot heal my backache, then I visit an acupuncturist. Our problem may be that we too uncritically accept the so-called established knowledge. When a doctor fails to cure the sickness of a patient, he or she rarely questions the medical body of knowledge. Rather, s/he questions his or her own expertise. Modern form of education posits a dumb learner and a smart body of established knowledge. From a Buddhist perspective, it is time that we question some of the fundamentals of the enlightenment in order to be enlightened.

To this end, we explore a proper methodology needed to "educate ourselves". Four themes central to Buddhist approaches to education can be drawn: (1) suffering (*dukkha*) exists; (2) *dukkha* finds its source in ignorance (*avidyā*); (3) ignorance can be resolved; and (4) there is a methodology to help us resolve ignorance.

## Threefold Training (*Tiśkṣā*)

Of course, this process of education requires the cultivation of both the intellect and the emotions or sentiment. Put differently. in Buddhist education the intellect and the emotion/ sentiment must develop concurrently, and praxis must be in congruence with society, facilitating an understanding of life and the world that is not marred by prejudices, selfishness, etc. This is the essence of education for liberation. For Buddhists, the objective of the highest stage of training is liberation from the ignorance that enshrouds human beings. This liberation opens the way to wisdom; that is, understanding the truth (the way it is) of everything without prejudices or attachments. At this stage, understanding would blend with compassion. Thinking and emotion are inclined towards compassion. Helping other human and sentient beings becomes an endless personal mission.

One must inevitably observe, understand, and solve individual and social problems. This constitutes *śikṣā*, or education which seeks to combine wisdom and ethics.

At no other time in history is the importance of *śikṣā* in applying ourselves to resolving social and political failure more urgent than today. For centuries mankind has exhibited magnificent aptitude at manufacturing all sorts of interesting little things but never have we stopped to ask ourselves whether these things make us more secure or less secure. As Martin Luther King Jr. stated: "our scientific activity actually has putrun our spiritual power. We have guided missiles and misguided men."

Buddhism emphasizes ethics with education, while Western educational systems struggle to do so. G.E. Moore writes in his *Principia Ethica* that Western thinking not only cannot be used to teach ethics, it also cannot define morality or goodness. Buddhist education cultivates morality (*śīla*) along side wisdom (*paññā*): the one guiding the way for the other. Before wisdom can be grasped and ultimately used to benefit humanity one must have a proper perspective of the world (right view). Thus, the highest training in the Buddhist system is liberation from ignorance. At this stage understanding blends with compassion. Thinking and emotion are inclined towards compassion. To know or understand does not mean to dominate or possess others or contain their singularities. Helping other sentient beings becomes an endless personal mission.

*Śikṣā* or training entails developing oneself so that one is able to lead life in a beautiful and correct manner-pursuing the path (*magga*) that will lead to the cessation of suffering. *Śikṣā* and *magga* thus can be seen as one. At times the Buddha would use the word *patipadā* (mode of progress) interchangeably with *magga*. Ultimately, the path leads to a noble and celibate way of life. I feel that tertiary education for liberation must start with the concept of the Right Understanding, and then proceed down the Noble Eightfold Path, namely:

1. Right Understanding,
2. Right Thoughts,
3. Right Speech,
4. Right Action,
5. Right Livelihood,
6. Right Effort,
7. Right Mindfulness,
8. Right Concentration.

The Buddha grouped points 3, 4, and 5 as morality, points 6, 7, and 8 as concentration; and 1 and 2 as wisdom.

The Noble Eightfold Path is also called the Middle Way—the path towards liberation from the extremes of sensual indulgence and self-mortification. On the one hand, structural injustices in society are perpetuated by violence. On the other hand, they are also held in place by our selfishness—our tacit consent. Social and individual sufferings result from the interpenetration of external and internal causes.

As mentioned above, to overcome individual and collective forms of suffering, a Buddhist practitioner can resort to socially engaged Buddhism. At the individual level, Buddhism seeks to transform greed, hatred, and delusion into loving kindness and compassion. But to overcome individual suffering one must also be aware of the suffering emanating from social injustices, from structural violence. And to overcome social suffering, one cannot act as an island unto itself: one must cooperate with others. In other words, one must avoid the Scylla of hermetically sealed personal liberation, and the Charybdis of social transformation without cultivating loving kindness and compassion.

The training of the mind and of morality will help students to develop knowledge in tandem with goodness. As Wittgenstein mentioned, goodness and beauty are in fact one. If "ethics is transcendental" then it is also supramundane. And once students develop training in wisdom, they will understand things differently; different, that is, from what has always been taught in mainstream education. The training that constitutes the Noble Path is the threefold training (*tiśikṣā*): morality (*śīla*), mindfulness (*samādhi*), and wisdom (*paññā*).

## Wisdom (*Paññā*)

Wisdom is the recognition of the interdependence of things and of reality "that which is". This is the origin of the Right Understanding, which is the beginning of the Noble Eightfold Path. Conversely, with the Wrong View, one's thought processes and beliefs will always be wrong such as the mainstream value system that induces the tyranny of the "I" and its many offshoots.

The Buddha taught that Right Understanding has two main dimensions: external and internal. Externally are the voices of or warnings raised by others, especially those of virtuous companions. Internally is critical reflection—the ability to think, contemplate, analyse, etc. without prejudices, without personal attachments, resulting from mental training. With proper internal and external understanding we are better equipped to tread softly in the world.

Right Understanding will also help us see the flaws in traditional perspectives. For example, binarisms have long been utilized as useful tools for classification, for making sense of the world. But the problem is that there are few neutral binary oppositions: one pole is often privileged over the other. Say. white/non-white, modern/traditional, upper-class/lower class, us/them, developed/underdeveloped, and so on.

Shunning or being mindful of dualistic thinking, Buddhism can well take part in healing these oppositions that serve as sources of great sufferings in the world. To Buddhists, our minds are not simple mirrors that reflect the world. Rather, take part in constructing "reality". This does not mean that there is no world "out there", that everything is in our heads. It simply means that the "out there" does not have meaning in itself. We must give it meaning, and we often do so narcissistically. A rock, for instance, is not simply a rock. It can be a national boundary, a work of art, a prized geological formation, etc. Our processes of representing, ascribing meaning to, or relating to the "out there" are marred by greed, hatred, and delusion—with serious consequences. Buddhism urges us to be quick in recognizing and taking care of the prejudices involved in our knowing/knowledge of the world. At the very least, Buddhism urges us to reduce our prejudices, which are rooted in self-attachments and self-preservation. We must seek to understand the root causes that have created these effects.

## Morality (*Śīla*)

Although, the Buddha taught that *śīla* consisted primarily of right speech, right action, and right livelihood, I will for the sake of time encapsulate all three of these within the Buddha's teaching on generosity.

Generosity, or *dāna* in the Pāli language, may be seen as the foundation of education shared by every religion. And it is a subtle way of reducing self-attachments. We can say that generosity at the most rudimentary level means giving money or things. It requires helping the badly off by means that would not jeopardize the well-being of the better off. Such acts of generosity may be for particular ends—earning praise or goodwill, reserving a place in heaven, etc. Or it may be a completely selfless act. This level of generosity may be equated with primary education. Generosity at the level of secondary education means giving knowledge or truthfulness to a society that is full of lies. It entails speaking the truth to power, which may be basking in ignorance or prejudices. At the level of tertiary education, generosity means the absence of fear. Here, one no longer fears internal enemies such as greed, hatred, and delusion. How then could one fear external enemies? Without fear, one is willing and able to give and forgive. In the absence of fear (of death, personal security, etc.), one is in the position to perform noble deeds to society or to serve as a worthy model. Perhaps at this stage real distribution is also possible: giving to the badly off in a way that would impact significantly on one's well-being without however, making one worse off. Applying the concept of *dāna* to contemporary society, we may cultivate a consciousness that stresses giving more than taking. Humility, simplicity, and sufficiency—self-reliance—may consequently follow. And if one has an inclination for generosity and cherishes simplicity and humility—that is, stressing compassion and solidarity more than competition—one may begin to reclaim human dignity. In this case, it comprises having pride in local cultures and traditions, which are being overwhelmed by consumerism, modernity, and globalization. This is a Buddhist vision of a prosperous life.

## Mindfulness

The third factor in the Buddhist threefold training is mindfulness. "I breathe, therefore I am", might have been the Buddha's response to Descartes. Ultimately, Buddhism urges us to be "awake" or what is often called "enlightened". And being awake in part results from proper or mindful breathing. As it is cited numerous times before: according to a Buddhist story, a leader of a religious sect came to visit the Buddha one day and asked Him, "If I follow your Way, what will I do day by day?" The Buddha replied, "Walk, stand, lie down, sit, eat, drink". The religious leader the inquired "what is so special about your Way?" And the Buddha answered,

> "It is indeed special. The ordinary man, though he walks, stands, lies down, sits, eats, and drinks, does not know he is walking, standing, lying down, sitting, eating, and drinking. But when we walk, we know that we are walking When we stand, we know that we are standing."

Buddhism urges us to restructure our consciousness, to perceive the world non-judgementally, that is, without division and conflict.

Without mindfulness, moral training may bring about narrow-mindedness or hubris, that is, the certainty or feeling that one is better than those without morality. For example, those upholding the eight precepts may feel superior to those only practising the five precepts, and those upholding the 10 or 227 precepts may regard themselves as superior to all others. This is of course dangerous. The Buddha had warned against this tendency: the belief that one will attain purity and enlightenment by blindly practising or observing moral training is akin to heightening personal attachments, which will undoubtedly contribute to suffering.

The training of the mind will contribute to mindfulness; one will be quick in taking care of one's feelings, especially greed and hatred, and will have concentration in leading life. With mindfulness, one may learn to become less attached to oneself. Moreover, mindfulness contributes to happiness in the present. It enables the mind and the heart to operate synchronically, and may bring about internal peace. Additionally, mindfulness enables one to grasp the realities of the past, the present, and the future. And lastly, mindfulness enables one to overcome mental defilements, thereby contributing to liberation.

Unfortunately, the cultivation of mindfulness is a dimension missing from contemporary education. Mindfulness increases the capabilities or potentials of the mind, making it stronger, more stable, more courageous, more persistent, more diligent, and more responsible. And mindfulness helps increase virtue by fostering loving kindness, compassion, altruistic joy, and equanimity—all these, even at the moment when one is being exploited or oppressed. In other words, mindfulness entails cultivating the capability, value, and health of the mind, which are indispensable in modern society.

To conclude, Buddhist education shows us how to act ethically with wisdom and mindfulness. Such an education is valid not only in our personal affairs, but also in how we interact with the world. This means that we must confront those causes that are linked to the abuses of capitalism and consumerism. To profess faith in the sciences and industrial technologies without questioning their ethical value or our moral responsibility could have serious consequences in our immediate future.

## REFERENCES

Conze, Edward (1954). *Buddhism: Its Essence and Development.* New York: Philosophical Library.

Coomarswamy, A.K. (1928). *Buddha and the Gospel of Buddhism.* London: Harper Textbooks.

Kalupahana, David J. (1976). *Buddhist Philosophy: A Historical Analysis.* Honolulu: University of Hawaii Press.

Keith, A.B. (1923). *Buddhist Philosophy in India and Cylon*. Oxford: Clarendon Press.

Moore, G.E. (1993). *Principia Ethica*. London: Cambridge University Press. First Revised Edition.

Murti, T.R.V. (1960). *The Central Philosophy of Buddhism*. London: George Allen & Unwin.

Rahul, Walpola (1959). *What the Buddha Taught*. New York: Grove Press.

Rhys Davids, C.A.F. (1932). *A Manual of Buddhism*. London: Sheldon Press.

Thomas, E.J. (1951). *History of Buddhist Thought*. New York: Berns and Noble.

# 17

# Value Education

## The Need of the Our Hour

*Sohan Raj Tater*

Samuel P. Huntington in his book *The Clash of Civilization and the Remaking of the World Order* (Touchstone Edition, 1997: 380-82) considered as "one of the most, important books to have emerged since the cold war" writes:

> "Far more significant than economics and demography are problems of moral decline, cultural suicide, and political disunity in the West. Oft-pointed-to manifestations of moral decline include:
>
> 1. increase in ant-social behaviour, such as crime, drug-abuse, and violence, generally; and
> 2. family decay, including increased rates of divorce, illegitimacy, teenage-pregnancy, and single-parent families."

How far to go with the moral decline and, its consequent punishments? Chinese government had to intensify punishment—killing of culprits in a society where religious values were either rejected or destroyed by a so-called godless communism for a few decades. Sweden is known by many as a "contraceptive society". To the Westerners Vivekananda exposed the sad results of a purely intellectual culture. The majority of students today simply do not have a higher purpose of life, beyond personal profit, money-making, power-grabbing, and sensate enjoyments. This "economic reductionism ends in a Hedonistic Paradox by which peace eludes even after repeated sensate pleasures". Then begins a feeling of deeper frustration and purposelessness when the left-brain educated person begins to suffer from Noogene Neurosis, a sense of guilt for all the inhuman pleasures and cut throat cheating he/she had to pursue to achieve their goal. Third wave civilization as Toffler calls it, "must also begin proving a framework of order and purpose in life". Perpetual purposelessness leads a young man to heroin addiction, which temporarily gives a way of life to a young person.

The UNESCO report admits that the sense of depression and frustration among the youth is due to "a distorted vision of man and the Universe". The dominant Western view is—man is a born sinner, and life is meant for sensate pleasures. The Vedāntic view is that man is a born "God" and all the activities of life should help him to manifest his/her innate perfection and divinity, attainment of Zatori and Buddhahood, as Zen masters would say. UNESCO recommends Education To BE. Education to be what? Vedānta answers—education to be the infinite man, the complete man, the Christ-Buddha Man.

Inculcation of values is a struggle to bring out the God from out of the animal man. Sometimes, it is a life-long struggle. Values cannot be taught in a day. It requires the entire education period right from elementary education to that of research to infuse values in learners. A century ago Swami Vivekananda cautioned Indians in 1897: "We must have a hold on the secular and spiritual education of the nation. Till then there is no salvation of the race."

## Value Education

Value education is going to emerge as a new science for inspiring human values in our highly scientific and technologically advanced society. The challenge in front of today's techno-globalism is the creation of value-based human beings. Einstein's brain should be combined with Buddha's heart to stop the devastation of Nagasaki and Hiroshima. Napoleon's dynamism should be combined with Vivekananda's prophetic passion for helping human beings to manifest their divinity and Rāma-Kṛṣṇa's universal love, respect and acceptance of all religions, should be combined with the spirit of intense religious revival which is emerging all over the world today.

## Value Education: The Vedāntic Vision

According to Vedānta philosophy, which is the highest culmination of Vedic knowledge, the human personality consists of five layers or sheaths. These five sheaths are: 1. The physical body (*annamaya-kośa*), 2. vital body (*prāṇamaya-kośa*), 3. mental body (*manomaya-kośa*), 4. intellectual body (*vijñānamaya-kośa*), and 5. blissful body (*ānandamaya-kośa*). In the West, man is a body; he has a soul. In India man is basically the non-physical self, which takes a body according to desires of the evolving soul. A purely technical education can cover the first four layers. It can physically, mentally, and intellectually energize the students, but can never touch the final non-physical spiritual self, which is the source of infinite bliss, knowledge, strength, and all kinds of human excellence hidden within each and every student.

## Value-Based Lives Inspire Values

The *Bhagavadgītā* III.21 speaks of the tremendous influence exerted by great value-based lives: "Whatever the greatest men of society do, common masses imitate. Whatever the great ones prove by their actions, others follow unconditionally."

> *yat yat ācarati śreṣṭāni, tat tat eva itaro janaḥ* |
> *sa yat pramāṇam kurut lokaḥ tat aṇuvartate* | |

The Socratic dialogues of Plato revolved around the question, "Can value be taught?". He realized that virtue is universal and is always the same everywhere; that the good values can be taught, but teachers must be good, such teachers "call out" our inherent virtues rather than instruct us. While words teach values: great persons inspire us to put them into practice.

## Historic Examples of Value-based Lives

World history provides us with some of the most inspiring examples of value-based lives who reached historic excellence.

King Aśoka flooded the Kaliṅga fields with human blood for the fulfilment of his ambition to conquer that kingdom. Out of intense remorse and penitence at the sight of the dying thousands, he found solace in a Buddhist monk who taught him non-violence, love, and service as the way to true fulfilment and peace. Aśoka started a new life of conquest through *dharma* (*dharma vijaya*), and emerged as great king.

Guru Govind Singh saw his own father Guru Tegh Bahadur being beheaded in Delhi Chandani Chowk. Yet he did not stop to fight the mighty Mughals. Even when distrusted and resisted by Hindu princes, Govind Singh continued fighting for India's eternal religion. His sons and his wife were killed most brutally by the Mughals. Undaunted, Govind Singh fought again and finally got treacherously stabbed by the enemy. He died leaving behind the great force of Sikhism where the final leader—as Govind Singh taught—is not any individual, but the *Guru Granth Sahib*. His immortal slogan, "Sardār-Sirdār" he who sacrifies is the leader and his historic sacrifice gave birth to sentinels of India's religion—the Sikhs, the heroes from the land of Punjab.

American Tycoon Rockefeller met Vivekananda in USA who told the rich man to find fulfilment by offering his wealth for impoverished have-nots. Rockefeller took the message of Vivekananda.

Rockefeller wrote at the end of his life:

> "There is more to life than the accumulation of money.... The best way to prepare for the end is to live for others. That is what I am trying to do."

## Holistic Action and Self-control: The Indian Ideal for Kings

What is righteous action? All righteous action is based on the holistic truth—I and my brother are one—action, which is meant for the good of many, for the welfare of many, Cāṇakya's aphorisms inspired Indian kings to seek success in administration by this time-tested method of righteous action leading to the manifestation of divinity within:

- *Sukhasya mūlam dharmaḥ* (The root of happiness lies in righteous action).
- *Dharmasya mūlam artham* (The root of *dharma* is the legitimately earned wealth).
- *Arthasya mūlam rājyam* (The root of such wealth lies in having a kingdom).
- *Rājasya mūlam* (*śāsakasya*) *indriya vijayam* (The root of kingdom lies in the self-controlled life of the ruler).
- *Indriya vijayasya mūlāt vinayam* (The root of self-control lies in genuine humility).
- *Vinayasya mūlam vṛddhopasevā* (Humility comes from serving enlightened persons).
- *Vṛddhopasevāya vijñānam* (From the service of enlightened persons comes wisdom).

- *Vijñānena ātmānam sampadyeta* (By wisdom is gained the knowledge of the *ātman*—Self).
- *Sampaditātma jitātma bhavati* (A man of self-realization conquers everything in the universe).

## Sardār-Sirdār: He Who Sacrifices is the Leader

Vivekananda asserts that a mere awakening of an intellectual, dynamic of intelligent man is never enough. Success comes only when the holistic personality, inspired for serving others also emerges along with the intellectual man. Guru Govind Singh's slogan has been immortal in India: "Sardār-Sirdār".

Young executives or leaders today develop ego-centred devotion to the organization and seek status symbols like promotions, honours, titles, and positions of power. Vivekananda plunged himself down to absolutely menial activities like cleaning big utensils of cooking, and even cleaning old-time latrines of the first Ramakrishna Math when workers failed to turn out. "If you want to lead, first serve others", he taught. To the Mahārāja of Mysore; Vivekananda wrote the inspiring words (letter dated 23 June 1884):

> "My noble prince, this life is short, the vanities of life are transient, but they alone live who live for others, the rest are more dead than alive."

## Unselfish Action Brings Success

Gāndhārī, the symbol of righteous knowledge, advised her son Duryodhana before the war to accept the path of righteousness or *dharma*, but Duryodhana refused to listen to his mother. In the *Mahābhārata*, Gāndhārī cautioned her extremely brilliant son Duryodhana and said (Udyoga Parva, 128.21.2.30):

*na hi rājyam mahāprajña svena kāmyena śakyate*

*apitum rakṣitam vā api bhoktum vā bharatarṣaba* |

*vaśyendriyam jitātman dhṛtadaṇḍam vikāriṣu*
*parīkṣakāriṇam dhīram atvaśam śrī nasevate* | |

> "O my extremely brilliant and mighty son, no one can get a kingdom if he fights only for his personal benefit; even if he gets it, he can neither keep nor enjoy it. Unless the leader is self-controlled, the assistant ministers will never listen to him, nor can he give punishment to evildoers if he takes rash decisions with an unsteady mind. The Goddess of Wealth never comes to such a person."

## REFERENCES

Burke, M.L. (1989). *Swami Vivekananda in the West*, Vol. 1, pp. 478-88, Advaita Ashrams, Calcutta.

*Challenge of Education*. New Delhi: Government of India, 1985, pp. 15-25.

*Complete Works of Swami Vivekananda*, Vol. 1, p. 124; Vol. 3, pp. 114, 277, 301, Vol. 9, p. 221.

*Learning to be,* UNESCO, 1972, pp. 154-55, 157.

Lincoln at Gettysberg by George Wills, p. 52.

*National Policy on Education* (1986), p. 195.

*Reminiscences of Swami Vivekananda* (1992). Advaita Ashrama, pp. 2-7.

Sikhion (1969). *Punjab Patiala*, p. 106.

*The Third Wave*. Alvin Toffler, p. 95.

William and Herman: *Einstein and the Poet Branden*. Press Brooklyn USA, p. 66.

# 18

# Need of Value Education in Modern Era

*Sohan Raj Tater*

The forces of globalization, the lifting of boundaries through immigration, and the transmission of ideas and cultures made possible through technology and transportation have produced a new religious pluralism and cultural multiplicity in countries throughout the globe. Within this increasingly pluralistic, interdependent world, we have also seen develop a global climate of religious mistrust and animosity, a climate that has spawned intolerance, discrimination, hate crimes, and other forms of violence. In response to our current world, many educators have begun to ask where education is taking us and how it is addressing the most pressing problems of our time. As Jacques Delors, head of UNESCO's International Commission on Education, states:

> "In confronting the many challenges that the future holds in store, humankind sees in education an indispensable asset in its attempt to attain the ideals of peace, freedom, and social justice. The Commission does not see education as a miracle cure or a magic formula opening the door to a

> world in which all ideals will be attained, but as one of the principal means available to foster a deeper and more harmonious form of human development and thereby to reduce poverty exclusion, ignorance, oppression and war."[1]

Education is our hope for the future, and many progressive educators recognize that it is no longer enough to meet only the intellectual needs of students. They understand that nurturing productive citizens requires a holistic approach that takes into account the intellectual, emotional and spiritual dimensions of persons. Value education methodologies and curricula focused on exploring and developing values, attitudes, and behaviours in constructive and creative ways—has arisen as a response to the challenges of the twenty-first century. As educators strive to meet these challenges, they must also recognize the critical role religious identity and culture plays in our world. Religious traditions have exerted a formative influence on all of the world's civilizations and they continue to affect the global community in both positive and negative ways.

Today a growing number of educators, practitioners, and religious leaders are turning to interfaith education as a means of illuminating and responding to these challenges. Broadly defined, the emergent field of interfaith education seeks to investigate and refine our knowledge of the interreligious dimension of human affairs. Within its scope lie the educational methods of the classroom, the academy, and the seminary, along side the restorative practices of dialogue, community building. Consciousness-raising and cooperation among people of diverse religious backgrounds. Interfaith education incorporates curricula and methodologies that are constructed to teach individuals about religious traditions outside of their own. Interfaith education enables us to deepen our understanding of our own traditions, engaging both the commonalities that bring us together and the particularities that make us distinct. Interfaith education not only fosters respect for those who are different from us, but also encourages us to look at our traditions with new eyes. In particular, interfaith education is challenged to address the hegemonic tendencies of religions, through which some traditions have dominated or oppressed others; the histories of violence found within many of our religious traditions; and the exclusivist and triumphalist strands within religious traditions that promote intolerance, discrimination, and even violence. The value of interfaith education is that it enables one to become aware of the importance of religious traditions, and of ritualizing and celebrating the sacred. The experiential and necessarily self-reflective nature of interfaith education creates the capacity for profound personal and societal growth, which is essential for fostering and sustaining cultures of peace.

In this chapter, we will look at the origins and complex development of interfaith education, specifically focusing on the evolution within our own organization, the Temple of Understanding. The strengths of interfaith education have developed through over 100 years of grassroots interfaith work; within this context we will examine the lessons learned and the underlying values implicit in this work, and briefly consider how interfaith education can enrich values education.

## Interfaith Education: Origins and Development

The interfaith movement ostensibly began in 1893 at the World's Parliament of Religions gathering in Chicago. This vent was the first time that leaders of "Eastern" and "Western" religions had come together to dialogue. Although, the organizers of this event were not able to sustain an ongoing organization, the World's Parliament inspired the eventual formation of oganizations set to meet and cultivate dialogue among people of the world's religions. At its onset, the organizations within the nascent interfaith movement sought to bring together religious and spiritual leaders of diverse traditions to dialogue, to educate each other and their audience about their respective traditions, and to introduce so-called "Eastern" religions to the "West". These organizations convened conference and summits to bring these leaders together with eager and interested lay people.

In 1900, a group called the International Council of Unitarian and Other Liberal Religious Thinkers was formed. This group eventually became known as the Interfaith Association of Religious Freedom. An early Executive Director, Diether Gehrmann, described how imperative personal experience is in religious education: "illuminating personal experience is the formost motivational and educational factor in religious life".[2]

The next interfaith organization to arrive on this early scene was the World Congress of Faiths (WCF) in the United Kingdom in 1936. The founder Sir Francis Younghusband, a true visionary documented his experience thus: "there was a burning within me and I felt in touch with the flaming heart of the world ... a mighty joy-giving power was at work in the world ... and in every living thing."[3] Younghusband's experience of a divine or ultimate force that transcended the limitations of religious boundaries had a profound impact upon the mission of the WCF. Yet, WCF promoted a vision of a reality where all religions peacefully coexist and maintain their diversity. Their conferences upheld the important role of personal spiritually transformative experiences in religious education.

In 1960 another visionary, Juliet Hollister, created the Temple of Understanding (TOU). Her vision came to her with the recognition that the world was in grave danger unless the gifts, wisdom, and insights of religious traditions could be recognized and cultivated to promote positive social change. Hollister began to develop her idea, by appealing to Eleanor Roosevelt and making a trip around the world to gather support for what became the TOU.

The TOU focused on summits that brought the leaders of the world's religions together to examine problems of intolerance, injustice, and persecution for religious beliefs worldwide. Soon the TOU organized regional conferences in the United States at Princeton, Harvard, and Cornell universities. This was in the 1970s—D.T. Suzuki, Alan Watts, Chogyam Trungpa, Chitrabhanu, and Swami Satchidananda were introducing Buddhism, Jainism, and Hinduism to Americans. This influx of Asian religions in the US opened up the scope of religious possibilities for American students. Consequently, these conferences created a buzz on college campuses—an average of 1,500 students walked out of their classes to "sit-in" on the TOU conferences. Clearly, a spiritual hunger in the US welcomed the arrival of religious teachers from Asian countries, and the TOU was perfectly situated to translate this into an interfaith movement. The TOU thereby became one of the pioneering organizations of the interfaith movement.

Drawing from the origins of the interfaith movement, organizers began to articulate a model of religious education that placed great value on empirical knowledge. Once inter-religious literacy within the interfaith movement was established, organizers began to focus their attention on the most effective methods and pedagogics for teaching others about different religions. Thus, the field of interfaith education began to emerge. The traditional conference model was soon joined by more personal and experiential models of community visits, service learning and immersion experiences.

Indicative of how approaches to interfaith education have expanded from the origins of the interfaith movement, the TOU has recently initiated a multi-year endeavour entitled "Consultations on Interfaith Education". Beginning in 2002, the TOU came together with other like-minded organizations to map the emerging field of interfaith education. The result of our initial collaboration was a conference series—the first and second held in New York in January 2002 and March 2003, the third in Atlanta in November 2003, and the fourth upcoming at the July 2004 Parliament of the World's Religions in Barcelona, Spain. Co-hosted by the member organizations, the consultations have assembled an international body of representatives from the educational, religious, social service and diplomatic fields in order to exchange ideas, practices, information, and resources. They have comprised a pioneering effort to navigate the complex landscape of interfaith education, identifying both its problematic and promising features, with the goal of reaching new horizons in practical problem solving, peace-making, and tolerance through education. These conferences have revealed that many organizations are working with interfaith education, but without the organizational support structures that would connect them as a field and lend coherence and momentum for growth. In response, our collective organizations are currently engaged in a project to provide integrated support structures and services to develop the field of interfaith education.

The TOU uses its local educational initiatives as models for continued research into exceptional programmes for a variety of settings. The mission of the TOU has evolved into a commitment to excellence in developing the emerging and important field of interfaith education.

What we have written is by no means a complete history of the interfaith movement. Since 1993, the Parliament of the World's Religions has, organized major gatherings, one in Chicago, a second in Cape Town, South Africa, and a third coming up in Barcelona, Spain. The United Religions Initiative began soon after 1995 and is now a substantial network of Cooperation Circles around the world. Organizations across the United States are engaged in this important work, including the Long Island Multi-faith Forum (a grassroots interfaith awareness programme for Long Island residents), the Chicago-based Interfaith Youth Core (a faith-based community action programme for area youth) and Seeking Common Ground/ face to face. Faith to Faith in Denver (a reconciliation programme for adolescents from the Middle East, South Africa. Northern Ireland, and the United States). These programmes demonstrate the practical value of interfaith education, offering hope for future educators, leaders, and adherents of all faith traditions.

## Interfaith Education: Methodology and Praxis

The process of expanding and promoting the field of interfaith education is ongoing. Underlying these efforts are the ethical imperatives of responsible citizenship in the emerging global village peace-making, tolerance, and mutual understanding. Within the objectives of interfaith education, many values are implicit. They include: community and solidarity, self-awareness, mutual respect and understanding and citizenship. Let us now look at these values in depth.

Honouring the differences and the uniqueness of cultures is a central aspect of interfaith cooperation and understanding. While interfaith organizations have been careful to acknowledge the particularities of religious traditions and honour their diversity, they have been accused of syncretism or of attempting to create a new religion of interfaith. This challenge has been seminal to interfaith education, as it is important for interfaith organizations to illuminate how religions of the world share common spiritual values, and yet, it is important to make clear that interfaith is not advocating syncretism or one world religion. Rather, interfaith education looks for the morals and values in each religious tradition and tries to understand them in terms of their history and cultural identity. This practice entails honouring the diversity of each religious tradition. The purpose of interfaith work is to develop a paradigm that promotes and achieves a peaceful interreligious dynamic. As each tradition looks at its own shortcomings and judgemental attitudes, it is enabled to shift toward an enhanced degree of respect for other faiths.

In our efforts to try to understand beliefs and traditions different from our own, we often examine and reflect upon our own belief system, and thereby discover new aspects of ourselves in the process. Engaging the beliefs of others often illuminates our own belief system, and makes us aware of aspects of our own traditions we have taken for granted or do not truly understand. Essentially, when we take time to explore and engage the diversity of the world around us, we find our worlds are far richer. Interfaith education advocates for an appreciation of diversity within our communities and society, but also for an appreciation of the diversity within religious traditions. Religions, are not monoliths, but rather have been shaped in dialogue with local cultures and immediate contexts, and are therefore complex and internally varied.

Community is a central value to interfaith education, as the practices emphasize engagement, relationship and community building. At the core of the interfaith endeavour is the quest to create a culture of peace. Interfaith education seeks to foster knowledge, respect, and understanding so that people find comunon values, beliefs, and experiences. The relationships and community built through these encounters are foundational to constructing a culture of peace. Moreover, interfaith education questions whether religion can ever be studied objectively, and instead asserts that we can only understand religious traditions through the lenses of our own religious experiences. Therefore, it is best to approach religious studies with this in mind, to unpack our own assumptions, and to work to create a dialogue between our own tradition and those we engage.

Self-awareness is a value which has great emphasis placed on it, as inerfaith education is grounded in the assumption that we all hold the potential for self-actualization. The methodological praxis involved with interfaith education pushes us to consider new ideas and challenges us to reconsider our views of the world and ourselves. Interfaith education seeks to create a just and compassionate community. Maintaining a world view where one's identity has rigid boundaries and is threatened by difference proves difficult to maintain in our pluralistic-global society. When we view the world from this perspective, we find ourselves in a constant state of tension and conflict, and feel threatened by that which we do not know or understand. In this pluralistic world, we must develop more fluid identities that can coexist as well as be enriched by differences in culture, ethnicity, race, gender, class, and, religion.

The kind of openness that interfainth education promotes requires mutual respect in order to be effective. In order to feel affirmative about the differences that exist among us, one must also feel that others return that respect and understanding. Such affirmation is often experienced and expressed during interfaith educational programmes. The best models of interfaith education are experiential. Effective models of interfaith education allow participants to gain understanding of traditions outside their own through opportunities to see religious traditions in practice in authentic settings.

The TOU's youth interfaith education programme, "Dialogue in Action" is one example of experiential programming common in interfaith education pedagogy. This youth programme places an emphasis on interfaith understanding through relationship and community building. Over the course of a year, young people aged 15-19 from different religious backgrounds spend one day a month visiting the communities of their peers. Through this programme, they observe the practices and customs of eight religious communities while expanding and clarifying their own sense of religious identity.

Truly interactive programmes such as "Dialogue in Action" provide participants and educators with an occasion to ask questions and exchange views in a dynamic and exciting format. Most interfaith educational programmes aim to put a "face" on religion, so religions are not explored in just an abstract, objective manner, but are experienced as values, beliefs, practices, and heritages that give meaning to the lives of people we know. Programmes such as these widen the scope of religious possibilities and understandings among participants. Presenting the complexities and internal diversity within religious traditions is the most effective means of dispelling stereotypes and preventing inaccurate generalizations and assumptions that can lead to bias and discrimination.

"Best practices" also promote the cultivation of leadership skills, public speaking skills, critical thinking skills, and dialogue skills. They connect these skills and knowledge to idea of citizenship and they encourage participants to explore how their religious identities call them to respond to the needs of their communities and the world. Interfaith education programmes provide participants and educators with an opportunity to ask questions and exchange views a dynamic and exciting format. More importantly, participants learn invaluable leadership skills and hone qualities that will remain important throughout their personal and professional lives, thus emphasizing the positive values implicit in the concept of citizenship.

Hopefully, this discussion has illustrated that "best practices" of interfaith education can illuminate the goals and objectives of values education. As an example, Living Values Education, a well-established values education programme endorsed by UNESCO, organizes its curriculum around twelve core values: "Cooperation, Freedom, Happiness, Honesty, Humility, Love Peace, Respect, Responsibility". Simplicity, Tolerance, and Unity.[4] These principles are also addressed and promoted within interfaith educational curricula. Interfaith educational programmes may even further illuminate these values by encouraging students to consider the place of these values within their religious traditions. The experiential element of interfaith educational programme enables practitioners and participants to access the enriching and transforming possibilities that arise when they learn to connect their belief systems with lived experiences.

Examining the history of the interfaith movement illuminates how values of peace and understanding lie at the core of the movement, and demonstrates how that history has influenced the pedagogy of interfaith education today. Interfaith education is inherently values education. Not only does it foster and promote a culture of peace by placing an emphasis on the benefits of diversity, as well as teach acceptance, respect, and mutual understanding of religious traditions outside of one's own, but it also has the ability to profoundly affect individuals by encouraging and enabling the process of self-transformation. Interfaith education is also necessarily experiential, thereby allowing it to be an innovative, engaging, and powerfully unique educational process, capable of enforcing positive change at both the global and individual level.

## NOTES

1. Delors, Jacques, *et al.* (1996). *Learning: The Treasure Within, Report to UNESCO of the International Commission on Education for the Twenty-first Century*. UNESCO Publishing.
2. Braybrooke, Rev. Marcus and James M. Gustafson (1992). *Pilgrimage of Hope: One Hundred Years of Global Interfaith Dialogue*. Crossroad/Herder & Herder, p. 61.
3. *Ibid.*
4. *Living Values Education*, http://www.livingvalues.net/aims/index. Html, April 2004.

# 19

# Peace Education and Value Education vis-à-vis Sustainable Development

*Sohan Raj Tater*

Peace and value education means providing education for internalizing appropriate values, attitudes, and behaviours with a view to respecting human dignity and right and respecting the environment.

Peace does not entail only the absence of conflict, but it requires a positive dynamic participatory process where dialogue is encouraged and conflicts are resolved in a spirit of mutual understanding. Respecting life, ending violence and promoting and practising non-violence through education, dialogue, and cooperation can help in establishing a culture of peace while ending a culture of violence.

UNESCO, which is committed to ensuring a culture of peace, believes that education plays an important role in fostering a culture of peace. Following are some of UNESCO's suggestions through which education can help in establishing a culture of peace.

- Invigorate national efforts and international cooperation to promote the goals of education for all, with a view to achiev human, social, and economic development and for promoting a culture of peace.
- Ensure that children from an early age, benefit from education on values, attitudes, modes of behaviour and ways of life to enable them to resolve any dispute peacefully and in a spirit of respect for human dignity and right.
- Involve children in activities for instilling in them the values and goals for a culture of peace.
- Develop values and skills conducive to a culture of peace, including education and training in promoting dialogue and consensus building.

Violence is emerging in an unprecedented manner in society. We expose our children from the very cradle to be competitive and aggressive. When these children grow up to be an adult. Thus have no qualms about lumping queues, driving rashly, abusing, getting violent or destroying the environment. It is not only we, as parents that cultivate this aggressive attitude in our children, but the surrounding environment also as well encourages the children to become violent and selfish.

Violence in the form of terrorism, war crimes, injustice, oppression and exploitation are on the rise. The daily newspapers scream headlines of gory details on acts of violence. Very little space is given to peace activities. Therefore, print media has an important role to play, in mediatizing peace activities, just as they do immediately mediatizing violence.

Also violent films which depict the lifestyle of the dons, showing glaring pictures on the underworld sends wrong messages to our children. Colourful toy cars and educational games have been replaced by videogames, toy tanks, and a high degree of competivity and achievement orientation, therefore, giving rise to a typical child of today who is short tempered, impatient and who starts to believe that violence is not an aberration but a way of life and actumulation of wealth, no matter how it is achieved, is attractive. Therefore, electronic media has an important role to play in projecting peace and values on the screen.

This disorder and confusion in the society affects the innocent minds of our children. Children absorb the spirit of violence in this atmosphere and grow to be the perpetrators of violence in the next generation.

It is here that the schools and teachers have an important contribution to make. The formative years which they spend in school actually shape their thinking process. But what we find in schools all over the world is that education is being narrowed down into teaching of certain subject matter necessary only for passing the examination and entering job markets. Due to this subject centred and examination-oriented learning at school, the purpose and the beauty of education has been lost.

There is a growing realization in the world today that children should be educated in the art of peaceful living. As a result more-and-more peace concepts, attitudes, values and behaviour skills are being integrated into the school curriculum in many countries. There is also a renewed interest to develop peace-related disciplines.

Peace and value education is an attempt to bring about changes in the values, attitudes, and behaviour of the children. It is a remedial measure to protect children from falling into the ways of violence in society. It aims at the total development of the child. It tries to inculcate higher human and social values in the minds of children.

Peace and value education is the best vehicle to ensure that the next generation will have the skills, the knowledge and the motivation to create a peaceful environment. Children must be provided with the skills and knowledge to live in peace and to create mutual respect and understanding that will help them to transform their lives.

## What Should Peace and Values Education Entail?

*Knowledge:* We must learn to know ourselves, enhance our capacities, think positively and understand each other, who is different from us. This requires that the curriculum textbooks must be jointly revised, so that, they are free from hate messages, prejudices and distortions. It also means that all education systems should ensure that the basic knowledge of the world's main civilization, religion, and belief systems is transmitted to each generation and is geared to enhancing the inherent potential of the person.

*Understanding:* Intercultural understanding must be based on dialogue across whatever cultural divide exists. This requires contact, exchange and negotiations for which interactive skills are vital. The ability to live together involves practical competencies that must be learnt and re-learnt in all cultures.

*Sharing:* In order to bridge the gap between our cultural differences, we must cultivate shared values. The universal values of tolerance, human rights, non-violence and democracy are crucial, as is respect for cultural diversity and a culture of giving and taking, winning, and losing.

To reinvent peace, we have to re-educate our children and ourselves. This can be done by reorienting the teacher training programmes, to ensure the professionalism of every teacher and teacher educator as a peace and values educator. We need therefore, to take measures to inspire teachers, to motivate them in the promotion of peace values, using the subject matter of each curriculum.

There is a need to initiate functionaries of school management systems into peace education by providing with the enabling, environment to do so. Moreover, there is a need to influence the relevant authorities to ensure that mass media falls in line with the mission of peace education by recognizing social responsi-bility.

There is a further need to develop and execute monitoring and evaluation mechanisms for peace education programmes and build these in to new programmes.

Peace and values education must be based on existing subjects taught in classes. It is not enough to have a separate subject on peace and values education only. Instead peace education should be incorporated into each and every subject of the school curriculum, such as maths, history, geography, language as well as into sports. The texts of these subjects, while expanding knowledge of the subject could be adapted as appropriate, this playing in highlighting concepts of peace.

Teachers should use these texts in conjunction with their traditional, subjects to discuss peace values daily. By doing so, issues pertaining to peace will be taught to the students in every class, rather than just having a single class on peace education, where once the student leaves the class, its lessons will be forgotten. This may be deemed the best method for internalizing peace values through education.

It is important to note that values education means imparting universally respected values of tolerance, non-violence, democracy and human rights, giving and sharing, winning and loosing, and above all respect for human dignity and right, with respect for the planet. These values are important to contribute to a peaceful environment. On the other hand, peace education should build the capacities of individual to become peaceful person by thinking positively and thinking critically.

To this end, UNESCO has brought out a publication, "Learning the Way of Peace"—A Teachers Guide to Peace Education. This should ideally, be globalized. Such attempts, will help in gradually changing the values, attitudes, and behaviours of the children who will grow up to be responsible citizens of the world. They would act with due respect to human dignity and right and respect for the environment, which are the corner stones for peace and sustainable development, in the times to come. They would think twice as future leaders, before promoting arms trade and war economies to sustain the living standards of their respective countries.

However, we must note that it is not enough only to target peace through education. It is necessary to lobby with the decision-makers in public and private sectors that environment to peace must be ensured to supplement what is done in schools, in order to bring about sustainable human development.

The dialogue between culture and development needs fresh energy and purpose.

In this context, the challenges of global governance, cultural diversity, and democratic development cannot be addressed in a piecemeal manner. They must be taken up in a single framework In the past, the policies, values and agencies concerned with dignity and diversity have been developed separately from those concerned with poverty, technology and social equity. This state of affairs much change, for the following reasons:

First, there is a widespread recognition that development without participation is doomed to failure. Without enlisting the enthusiasm of the world's poorer and weaker groups in the task of their own empowerment, and without making space for their own ideas about freedom, dignity and power, the work of development becomes another exercise in the imposition of power upon the weak. What is more, the lack of involvement of ordinary people at the grassroots level, in defining the meaning, shape and design of developments in their own communities is probably a major factor in the limited successes of efforts to reduce both rural and urban poverty worldwide. Although, there has been a significant effort to emphasize participation, empowerment and inclusion as both means and ends in development policy, the obstacles to such commitments have been many, including the mindsets of technocrats, the ideologies of major lenders, the biases of local communities and the tear of local elites about losing power when women, children and weaker groups achieve "voice" in their own futures.

The violent upheavals of the last few decades (often in the name of ethnic purity or racial chauvinism) and the events of this past year remind us that for the poor and and disenfranchized populations of the world, there is a strong perceived link between their cultural exclusion and their economic marginalization. Thus, peace itself can become a casualty of market-driven development.

*Development*, in UNESCO's view, is a means of enhancing the relationship between material and spiritual well-being by stressing their reciprocity rather than just their simple complementarily. Many experts would agree that the record of development over the last few decades has not been uniformly positive. Some would agree that this is because development has itself been defined far too exclusively by tangibles, such as dams, factories, houses, food and water, although, these are undeniably vital goods. What we may call intangible development (which includes such issues as empowerment, participation, transparency, stakeholding and accountability) has only recently entered the discourse of development.

*Intangible development* may be defined as that, set of capacities that allows groups, communities and nations to define their futures in a holistic and integrated manner, stressing such values as participation, transparency and accountability. Intangible development, defined in this manner, is the critical link between cultural diversity and sustainable development. Cultural diversity enriches the pool of visions, which mediate the relationships between meaningful pasts and desirable futures. The strength of this mediation provides a bridge to sustainability, since the major obstacle to sustainability has been the divorce between visions of tangible and intangible development.

Since human beings belong to the biological universe, but are often in a position to determine its future, they have a special obligation to assure that a proper balance is maintained between environmental health (especially biodiversity) and equitable development. In the era where markets and their logic seem to dominate global relationships, environmental concerns, market concerns and development concerns seem to be in constant tension with each other. In many parts of the world, there is a growing gap between environmental values, which are seen as middle class or even elite values, and the needs of the world's poor for shelter, food and employment. For example, the efforts in India's West Coast to preserve a carefully regulated environ-mental zone along the coast is being contested by groups of urban poor who are desperate for spaces in which to construct secure housing. Therefore, the means of accessing knowledge to have a balanced interaction with nature, must now be increasingly provided to the populations.

The main arguments for the importance of biodiversity are grounded in the reality that the earth does not have an infinite capacity for being abused and the global commons depend on the preservation and nurture of biodiversity, at all environmental scales. Though many long-term factors have contributed to the environments degradation of the planet and the atmosphere, the historical trend towards more powerful extractive technologies, more effective worldwide market integration, and more profit- oriented forms of market organization has generally sacrificed long-term productivity and equity, for short-term gains for specific populations.

The era of globalization poses common challenges to biodiversity and to cultural diversity, as well as to the special relationship between them. The growing autonomy of market processes (in combination with high-impact technologies) produces unforeseen risks to biodiversity and environmental safety. At the same time, globalization in its cultural most marketized forms threatens to erode and diminish more localized and historically vulnerable cultural forms, both within and across, societies.

The forces of global consumerism make it difficult for many societies to maintain their cultural dignity, as products, slogans and images of glamour, wealth and modernity flood in from outside sources. Global financial markets place heavy pressure on national governments to sacrifice; national cultural priorities in favour, of global competitive trends.

This shrinkage of the space for cultural creativity, dignity and innovation has dangerous implications for biodiversity as well. In both cases, a blind and monotheistic attachment to market principles tends to marginalize long-term values. Cultural diversity and biodiversity are both values of and for the long run. And cultural diversity guarantees the maximum range of visions of the good life within which relationships to nature can also be varied, specific, local, and self-sustaining.

Therefore, educating the future generations on preserving biodiversity, as also the cultural diversity of the worlds population, is deemed very important.

What has happened and what is happening today, are part of our inherited legacies. It is still not too late, to chart a path of peace and sustainable development for the future.

## REFERENCES

Burke, M.L. (1989). *Swami Vivekananda in the West.* Vol. 1, pp. 487-88, Advaita Ashrama, Calcutta.

*Challenge of Education* (1985). New Delhi: Government of India, pp. 15-25, 69.

*Complete Works of Swami Vivekananda*, Vol. 1. p. 124; Vol. 3. pp. 114, 277, 301; Vol. 9, p. 221.

*Learning To Bed* (1972). UNESCO, pp. 154, 155, 157.

Licoln at Gettysberg by George Wills, New York, p. 57.
National Policy on Education (1986), p. 195.
*Reminiscences of Swami Vivekananda* (1992). Advaita Ashrama, pp. 2-7,
*Sikhism* (1969). Punjab, Patiala, p. 108.
*The Third Wave*, Alvin Toffler, p. 95.
William and Herman: *Einstein the Poet Branden*, Press Broklyn, USA, p. 66.

# 20

# On Creating the Ecologically Responsible Culture

*Archana Shrivastava*

One of the goals of environmental ethics is to describe and contribute to the creation of an ecologically responsible culture. The creation of such a culture requires the development of knowledge and abilities that will help sustain such a culture. Since education is one of the key institutions for instilling values and world views, it is important for environmental philosophers to think about the institutionalization of environmental theories in terms of their implications for the environmentally literate person. I argue that attention to literacy is significant for two reasons. First, it provides one way of evaluating the differences between competing environmental philosophies. Second, it raises the important question of what kind of person is required to carry out a particular vision of environmental responsibility. By addressing the issue of education and literacy, philosophers interested in environmental ethics can help create a vision of citizens who have democratically internalized and integrated environmental values and priorities rather than having them imposed from above.

Environmental ethics presents us with a plurality of different theoretical positions, from sophisticated forms of anthropocentrism to competing views of eco-feminism and social ecology to various versions of biocentrism. The ethical discussions these positions have prompted reveal how difficult it is to extend or revise existing moral traditions in a manner that appears both plausible and socially legitimate to mainstream audiences. Traditional human-centred world views have a strong hold on the minds and habits of action of citizens in Western industrialized societies, as well as in many others. Since the utopian goal of many philosophers interested in environmental ethics is the creation of an environmentally responsible and just culture, it is incumbent upon us to think critically about how various environmental ethical positions might be integrated with and institutionalized within the existing societies we know and experience.

Insofar as we frame one goal of environmental ethics to be the nurturing of an ecological culture, we must begin to ask how such a culture can be brought about. Clearly, environmental values and priorities must be institutionalized within a responsible society. But this suggests that environmental philosophy needs to examine the role to be played by education and educational institutions in the development of an environmentally responsible society. Education plays a major role in fostering the abilities and values of citizens. We should, therefore, ask how environmental aspirations ought to affect the goals of education.

I shall use the concept of "literacy" quite broadly to refer to the goals of the educational process. Environmental philosophers need to think through an image of the environmentally literate person as an integral part of doing environmental ethics. There are two reasons for saying this. First, environmental values must become an intimate part of the beliefs and aspirations of individual citizens if environmental responsibility is to grow in democratic soil and not from the imposition of what Andre Gorz refers to as "techno-fascism".[1] An environmental culture must also be a just culture in which citizens identify with and participate in the process of living a life in sustainable relationship to nature. We must, therefore, be concerned about how environmental values are incorporated into a vision of educational literacy.

My second reason for focusing on the issue of literacy and its links to environmental ethics has to do with ethics itself. One way to ramify and evaluate competing ethical theories about human relations to nature is to ask how these theories might be implemented in existing societies. What kind of person is required to carry out the particular ethical vision? What kind of educational system would be required to develop and sustain such people and give them the resources, motivation, and encouragement they need to be environmentally responsible, as this is understood by the theory in question? At the end of this chapter, I shall provide a brief example of how a difference in ethical viewpoint may have implications for a conception of literacy, and how this could help us to evaluate the relevance of the theory.

I have suggested that a conception of literacy is an important part of environmental ethics. But literacy is a problematic concept with a variety of definitions. Recent discussions in the United States have tended to define literacy either in functional terms, as the ability to read and write, or in cultural terms, as the mastering and possession of "cultural capital" needed to claim full membership in educated society. Neither of these approaches is particularly satisfactory for environmental ethics.

In my view, we need what might be called a "utopian" conception of literacy that reduces neither to the minimal functional requirements for living in contemporary industrial society, nor to the acquisition of the mainstream knowledge and aspirations of the cultural elites of already existing societies. From the perspective of environmental ethics and philosophy, the knowledge, aspirations, and dynamics of contemporary society are among the problems to be addressed by education, not the givens to which the educational system must accommodate itself.

As philosophers, our problem is to identify the theoretical framework within which we can think successfully about environmental literacy as an educational goal. The problem initially appears to be a question of knowledge; what do we need to know in order to sustain an environmentally responsible society? But this question is too narrow. I shall argue that a philosophically sound definition of environmental literacy will include more than access to certain kinds of knowledge and cognitive skills. It must help us to understand how to integrate knowledge with other aspects of the human person in an ecologically responsible fashion. Literate individuals must not only know, but they must be able to apply their knowledge in appropriate ways—that is, in the right way, at the right time, and with respect to the right situations, to echo Aristotle.

My assertion that more than knowledge is involved in the description of the environmentally literate person may appear problematic. But it is consistent with the claim of Aldo Leopold, one of the formative figures in the history of American thinking about the environment, that no important ethical change will take place "without an internal change in our intellectual emphasis, loyalties, affections, and conviction".[2] Leopold is correct, environmental literacy as an educational goal should contribute to changes in personal loyalties, affections, and convictions, as well as levels of scientific knowledge. Such an educational goal is utopian in the sense that it sets before us an ideal of integrated human thought, feeling, and action that is difficult to fully imagine, let alone achieve through the schools. It is an ideal that suggests the elimination of the kinds of internal conflict that are a familiar feature of everyday life.

A multi-dimensional conception of literacy also takes into account the emotional, perceptual, and motivational aspects of a person that play a crucial rule in our ability to interpret our experiences and arrive at intelligent decisions. As Lawrence Blum has noted, moral judgement in particular presupposes a process of moral perception that both defines the situation at hand and aids in the connection between situation, moral generalizations, and the concrete judgements and choices of the particular moment.[3] This framework can, of course, be extended to include non-moral contexts of judgement as well.

Environmental literacy in this full-blown sense becomes central to an environmental ethics because it draws our attention to the full range of human actions, beliefs, and emotions, and proposes that we seek the appropriate internal as well as external transformations needed for environmental sustainability and justice.

The need for this conception is apparent in the everyday experience of internal conflict in our own outlooks. Conflicts and confusion are no doubt part of the human condition. But in the context of the environmental crisis, the conflicts we experience between what we know and how we feel and act are particularly dangerous and require philosophical attention. We are well aware that people's speech and action frequently contradict each other. Indeed, I would argue that often what appear to be cases of weakness of will are instead symptoms of conflicting, but unresolved, commitments and judgements. For example, a person believes that automobile exhaust has negative effects on air quality, yet votes against taxes to increase public transportation and against policies that would restrict private use of cars. This individual's knowledge of the scientific facts fails to operate in their personal and political behaviour. At the same time, their personal and political choices reflect commitments that are not addressed by their scientific literacy. Similarly, a person who adamantly rejects the animal rights notion of a relevant similarity between human beings and non-human beings may betray this stated belief in their treatment of their pets or in their admiration of the abilities of some species of wild animal. As with the first case, the person here gives verbal judgements that differ from their actions and their actions express commitments that belie their verbal judgements.

My point is not to deny that an environmentally responsible society needs citizens with knowledge about how they affect the non-human environment. There is no doubt that some of the harms we have caused to the integrity of natural processes are due to ignorance of the nature and magnitude of our impacts. Better knowledge of materials, species, systems, and causal interdependencies is something that citizens, as well as politicians and professionals, should aspire to obtain. Environmental literacy does not, therefore, exclude this more traditional conception of literacy as knowledge.

But, at the same time, this is not enough. An environmentally responsible society also needs people able and willing to integrate their knowledge with their own expressive and practical commitments, preferences, and aspirations. If individuals remain fundamentally divided within themselves about where they stand on matters relating to the natural environment, sophisticated scientific discourse will not be sufficient to build a sustainable culture. A living culture presupposes the internal engagement of its members in many dimensions. Thus, knowledge must find support and coherence in action and expressive judgement too.

The American pragmatist philosopher, Justus Buchler, gives us one way to formulate the difficulties with a conception of literacy, even environmental literacy that is restricted to the cognitive, to knowledge and reason. According to Buchler, individuals make judgements that express their commitments and their position in the world in several different mode.[4] We usually associate "judgement" with verbal utterances, but Buchler argues that judgements also take the form of expressive contrivances or performances and actions. In the two examples mentioned earlier. The individual presents us with contradictory judgements, saying one thing and doing another. For Buchler, it is a mistake to privilege the verbal statement as conveying the person's definitive judgement. Instead, we should look for the source of the contradiction in outlook expressed by conflicting verbal and active judgements. It may be that the person is unaware of their conflicting beliefs. Or they may in fact be uncertain where they actually wish to stand on the issue.

Buchler's tripartite division of judgement makes it possible to see how a culture can complicate the educational process and thus, the hopes of attaining literacy. Not only may the students reveal conflicting and competing commitments themselves, through their speech, performances, and actions, but teachers and those with authority within the culture at large may do so as well. Thus, spoken adherence to freedom and equality may be accompanied with a demeanour or with overt actions that actively discourage or negate them. Similarly, even sincere verbal assurances of "green" sentiments often accompany actions that are merely environmentally destructive business as usual.

I would like to see environmental literacy formulated as an element of a utopian ideal in which knowledge, expressiveness, and action are consonant with one another. In order to do this, steps must be taken to root out what Brazilian educator, Paulo Freire, refers to as the voice of the oppressor, the voice naming values and ideals—reality in general—that is internalized by victims of oppression, but without their participation and in disregard for their interests.[5] In the case of environmental literacy. The "voice of the oppressor" is the voice of the mainstream of an anthropocentric consumer culture that is obsessed with economic growth at any cost. The "internal change" that Aldo Leopold talks about first requires us to combat this other internalized voice. The utopian ideal of an environmentally responsible literacy requires a person who can rid themselves of the internal conflicts that result from this inner voice which speaks in contradiction to scientific knowledge and environmentally inclusive moral aspirations. The literate person will be one who can reconcile their verbalized knowledge with their expressive productions, and with their overt active conduct. But to be able to do this, education must aim for more than just knowledge.

What more is needed for our utopian conception of environmental literacy, then, besides scientific literacy? Let me point to two distinct philosophical projects to answer this question. First, individuals must learn to develop a sense of relatedness to place and to the non-human environment. How we alter and shape the natural environment says a great deal about our understanding of our relationship to the non-human world. The built environment, in particular, is the product of human contrivance, that is, a human product that reveals our stance in the world. If we are to develop an environmentally responsible culture, we must become self-conscious about the judgements we make through our constructions, our shapings, and our improvements. If, as William James maintained, the meaning of our beliefs is found in the difference they make, then the meaning of our concrete relationships to place is revealed in the differences they make to the place itself as well as to our presence there. Public transportation routes that do not connect richer and poorer communities, zoning laws that permit development of wetlands, commercial development of fertile farmland, pollution of drinking water all reveal the difference our beliefs make about class structure or the value of nature. An ecologically responsible society must understand literacy—the goal of education—as extending beyond the verbal statements of specialized knowledge to the often contradictory manifestations of our beliefs in the products of human enterprise.

Second, I suggest that our relationship to place, together with our cognitive, expressive, and moral judgements must be integrated through new narrative structures that help us to formulate our expectations of how life and its various stages and forms is supposed to work out. Education aimed at environmental literacy must include attention to the need to revise our "naming" vocabulary and our moral narratives about the relationship between human beings and nature. Students and citizens must come to view their personal identities, their community boundaries, their employment aspirations, their recreational pursuits, and their political practices within the context of narratives that describe and portray sustainable relationships with nature. One of the tasks of environmental ethics may be seen here, namely, to articulate new narrative forms, new metaphors, and a new vocabulary for speaking about the world, expressing oneself within it, and acting to modify it. Environmental literacy can only be pursued in the light of these prior philosophical accomplishments, because our conception of literacy inevitably presupposes a particular set of philosophically articulated values and perspectives.

Any attempt to define a conception of environmental literacy—utopian as I have argued that it is—is complicated by the discourse of environmental ethics itself. Since literacy can only be defined relative to a vision of the goals to be attained by such educational achievement, the divisions within environmental ethics make a final analysis of environmental literacy as yet impossible. Clearly, eco-ferninists will emphasize different educational goals than utilitarians or deep ecologists. While the knowledge required for environmental literacy may remain relatively constant, the kinds and degrees of educational focus on our expressive and active judgement may very well vary significantly.

Time and the ultimately arbitrary delimitation of spatial boundaries make it difficult to remain satisfied with a fixed conception of intrinsic value or with a fixed set of educational aspirations. As Holmes Rolston has noted with respect to species, ecosystems, human communities, and indeed individual persons exist as temporal flower rather than as metaphysically fixed entities with clearly defined limits and membership.[6] Existing both in discrete forms and as tendencies and potentialities susceptible to chaotic interaction and change, both nature and human beings are dynamic forms not easily fixed without reference to specific purposes and needs.

The implications of this for environmental literacy—that is, for the project of thinking through the institutionalization and internalization of environmental ethical values—is significant. Increasing ecological knowledge, developing a sense of place, re-working the moral narratives that structure expectations and actions are goals that must be understood within a temporal framework. Rather than seeking to fix a specific content, our educational goal must be to acquire the cognitive, affective, perceptual, and practical abilities necessary to insert ourselves actively and sustainably into the temporal flow of existing human, communities, and natural ecosystems.

At the beginning of this chapter, I indicated that differences in philosophical theory would reveal themselves in their implications for education. The particular image I have just referred to, of inserting ourselves into the dynamic flow of an ecosystem or a human community, runs counter to some expressions of biocentrism, just as it runs counter to some expressions of conservativism in the political arena. It is true that conservative theorists of education understand cultural literacy as a kind of insertion into the existing community. The literate person becomes a member of the community by adopting and working with its prevailing ideas and norms. But such a perspective ignores the dynamic character of the community and seeks to prevent future change and evolution that conflicts with the interests expressed by the mainstream.

The biocentrist represents a different kin challenge. The biocentric path within environmental ethics is a reaction to the traditional devaluation of nature as an instrumental domain. To avoid reducing the value of non-human beings and systems to their use value for humans, the biocentrist argues for some form of intrinsic value that distinguishes nature in its own right. From a moral point of view, then, it becomes morally wrong to violate the intrinsic value of nature, especially those aspects of nature that remain wild and untouched by human activity. The logic of biocentrism calls for a hands-off strategy with respect to nature, humans should *not* insert themselves into the dynamic flow of ecosystems, because to do so is to change, domesticate, and humanize them.

In order to institutionalize the moral values of a "biocentric" environmental ethics we would need to develop cognitive, emotive, and perceptual skills that would enable us to withdraw as much as possible from active interaction with the non-human world. The literate person would be one in whom scientific knowledge was well integrated with expressive and active judgements that minimized or erased the human presence. At the present time, it is hard to see how such a vision of literacy could be institutionalized within our current culture in a just and democratic manner.

Time does not permit a full discussion of biocentrism or its alternatives. Since, I have suggested that environmental literacy should enable individuals to insert themselves into the dynamic flow of natural ecosystems in a responsible and sustainable fashion, it should be clear that I am not proposing a biocentric point of view. The contrast of the two positions may serve, however, to underscore the way in which one's ethical theory sets the agenda for one's conception of environmental literacy. It also suggests how we might use the topic of environmental literacy as a way of testing the fruitfulness of various positions in environmental ethics in more detail.

My goal in this chapter has been to present a case for thinking about environmental literacy as an element of environmental ethics. It may indeed be one way of reflecting on and evaluating the competing arguments and visions of the many theories currently discussed within the field of environmental ethics. I have argued, in addition, that when we do investigate the concept of literacy, we should acknowledge the dynamic character of individuals, communities, and nature itself. A utopian conception of literacy that holds up a prescriptive goal for the educational process should address not only our knowledge and I beliefs, but also our ability to make expressive and active judgements through our creations and our behaviour. This goal of an integrated stance in the world is crucial if we are to address the ambivalence, the contradictory impulses, and the confusion we now manifest in our approach to an environmentally responsible culture.

## NOTES

1. Andre Gorz (1980). *Ecology as Politics*. Boston: South End Press, p. 17.
2. Aldo Leopold (1966). *A Sand County Almanac, with Essays from Round River.* A Sierra Club/Ballantine Book: Oxford University Press, p. 246.
3. Lawrence Blum (1994). "Moral Perception and Particularity", in *Moral Perception and Particularity*. Cambridge University Press, pp. 30-56.
4. Cf. Justus Buchler (1955). *Nature and Judgement.* New York: Grosset and Dunlap, and *Toward a General Theory of Human Judgement* (2nd edn. 1951). New York: Dover Publications.
5. Paulo Freire (1983). *Pedagogy of the Oppressed*, tr. by M. Bergman Ramus. New York: Continuum, pp. 27-56.
6. Holmes Rolston III (1991). "Environmental Values in and Duties to the Natural World", in *Ecology, Economics, Ethics: The Broken Circle,* ed. Herbert Bormann and Stephen Kellert. New Haven: Yale University Press, pp. 82-96.

# 21

# Evaluation in Teacher Education is a Tool for Quality Sustainability

*Shashirekha S.M.*

## Introduction

Evaluation is an ongoing process that informs practice and contributes to the quality of provision from multiple perspectives. It is carried as part of the process of programme development to find out if everything is going on according to the plan or not. Teacher education institution has renewed interest in the attributes of evaluation systems used to guage their quality. Many systems are used with different purpose and consequences and also clarify their advantages and drawbacks. Due to this we need to use different evaluation techniques to sustain quality in teacher education. NCTE (1998) in quality concerns in secondary teacher education "The teacher is the most important element in any educational programme. It is the teacher who is responsible for implementation of educational process at any stage." Evaluation is an important in the process of gathering, utilizing and imparting all relevant and accurate information. It is a process of delineating, obtaining, and providing useful information for judging and makes decision. Quality makes education as much socially relevant as it is personally indispensable to the individual. It is not something that is bestowed by others, it is attained and maintained as a result of ceaseless efforts. Quality refers to "the totality of features and characteristics of the student teacher acquired as a result of the teacher education programme".

## Review of Related Literature

Review of related literature reveals the information about the evaluation empirical research on teacher evaluation shows that current practices do not improve teachers or accurately tell what happens in classrooms. A framework for teaching (Danielson, 1996) and how they will be assessed are central to the idea of tracher quality assurance. Professional growth must allow teacher the opportunity to reflect on their practice, work collaboratively with others in the profession and use self-assessment and self- directed inquiry (Danielson and McGreal, 2000). Research (Atkins, 1996, Brandt, 1996, Egelson, 1994) and experience suggest that without appropriate professional development opportunities, instructional support and guidance and proactive teacher evaluation and supervision any education restructuring effort is doomed to failure. In addition to classroom observations and evaluations by administrators, observation and critiques of teachers' performances other stakeholders are being seen more and more as a valuable part of a teacher evaluation instrument (Strobbe, 1993). Student ratings have been the largest traditional means of stakeholder's involvement the evaluation process during this century and are growing in popularity (Bonfadini, 1998; Lengeling, 1996; Strobbe, 1993; Williams and Ceci, 1997). Besides these some of the other evaluation techniques can be used to maintain quality in teacher education.

## Evaluation in Teacher Education

Evaluating the quality and effectiveness of teacher education programme is a necessary ingredient to improve teaching and learning. Exisitng evaluation are complex, varied, and fragmented however, it is necessary to use different techniques for evaluation. To know the impact of instruction on learning of students in their classroom and to shape, form or improve teacher performance evaluation is necessary. It helps teacher to improve their practices and to develop, use data, to inform, and judge teacher. Make decision about promoting, rewarding and give suggession to improve upon. To know the effectiveness of teaching, teacher strength and weakness, and find out the remedial measures. Whether the expectations of students, parents, and the society are met or not. Evaluation helps to make decision about teacher educators indirectly. It assists maintaining total quality in teacher education.

## Aspects of Teacher Education

Evaluation helps meet the needs of stakeholders. Effectiveness of delivery of educational process, management, leadership, and capacity to improvement are important aspects. Beside the aforementioned following aspects can be evaluated:

1. *Planning and Preparation:* Here knowledge of content and pedagogy is evaluated. It refers to what planning has the teacher done to demonstrate his/her knowledge of a particular subject by interrelating it with teaching skills. Whether the teacher has kept certain goals to teach in the class, to achieve these goals, how far teacher manages and utilize the resources and how he design for coherent instructions.
2. *The Classroom Environment:* Whether the teacher create an enviroment of respect and rapport in the classroom and with students. Teacher establishes a

culture for learning. Teacher can be evaluated on the basis of how far he/she manages class effectively and what techniques they use. How teacher could manage student behaviour and provided satisfactory seating arrangement in available classroom can be evaluated.

3. *The Classroom Instruction:* The teacher is expected to have good command over spoken language, whether teacher use variety of techniques in class like quesioning, discussion, demonstration, teacher engaging their students in learning throught broad outlines, objectives to be attained and selects materials and teaching aids suitable to their student level, feedback to students.
4. *Professional Responsibilities:* Effective teacher needs to fulfil these duties such as competence in the subject, attending seminars, workshops, conferences, etc. Teacher can conduct experimentation and research, or not.

## Principles of Evaluation to be Considered

1. *Evaluation should be carried continuously:* Teacher educators during their instruction continuously gather valid and reliable information about the performance of the learner on an ongoing basis. All the activities that take place during the teaching process should be evaluated. If teachers are continuously evaluated they get to know the level of learning of each and every learner in the class. They are able to offer support immediately when necessary and also provide suitable learning material to those who seem to be progressing well.
2. *Evaluation is a process not only product:* Evaluation is a continuous, progressive, and ongoing process. It means that teacher educators should evaluate at the end of teaching process as well as during the process.

This process is very important because teacher is able to identify their difficulty and find out solution for the same.

3. *Evaluation must be integrated with teaching and learning:* Teaching and learning go hand in hand. So, evaluation should be integrated into teaching and learning. Teacher educators should plan evaluation before any teaching begins and continue the evaluation till the end of teaching process.
4. *Evaluation must be authentic:* Evaluation must be authentic where teacher educators are allowed adequate time to plan, to complete the work, to evaluate themselves to revise and to consult others.
5. *Evaluation must be multi-dimensional:* In teacher education there are different aspects to be evaluated. So, teacher should use different evaluation techniques to evaluate various aspects of teacher education.
6. *All evaluation instruments should be convenient to administer:* Different instruments which can be used to evaluate teacher educators should be convenient to administer and clear to the evaluators.
7. *Evaluation should be well planned in advance:* In order to assess all the aspects of teacher education it is necessary to plan well in advance.
8. *All evaluation devices should be valid and reliable:* The devices which can be used to evaluate should be valid. They should measure what they intended to measure. They are realiable when produce consistent results over time.
9. *Evaluation should be impartial:* Evaluators should avoid personal prejudices. They should be impartial.

## Evaluation Techniques can be Used

Quality in teacher education can be sustained through the following ways:

1. *Annual Progress Appraisal Report:* It is one of the important techniques which can be used to evaluate detailed performance of teacher educators. It also helps to identify the strengths and weakness and to provide necessary suggestions.
2. *Student Rating:* This method can be used to evaluate teacher performance, knowledge of subject, skill, and attitude towards teaching.
3. *Classroom Observation:* Evaluation of teacher done through frequent observation of the class by experienced teacher. This technique reveals information about the teacher interaction and rapport with students.
4. *Student Achievement:* Through the student achievement teacher can be evaluated. It helps to evaluate teacher and institution systems by ranking the students.
5. *Teacher Interview:* Formal interview can be conducted according to the convenience of the institution with all the teachers. Through the interview teacher must actively interact with committee and present their performance and problems encountered in teacher education.
6. *Advisary-oriented Evaluation:* It means all evaluation in which there is a planned opposition in the points of view of different evaluators or evaluation teams. This type of evaluation enhances the confidance of teachers and make them responsible teacher educators.
7. *Expertise-oriented Evaluation:* Professional experts should judge an institution, programme and activity helps maintain quality in all the aspects.
8. *Consumer-oriented Evaluation:* Individual or independent agencies who take responsibility to gather information about educational or human service products. For example, curriculum packages, workshops, instructional media, inservice training opportunities, staff evaluation forms or procedures,

new technology, software, resources material, equipments, etc.

9. *Management-oriented Evaluation:* This is an essential part of good decision making, policymaking, boards, practictioner, etc. who need information.
10. *Faculty Self-evaluation:* It helps to reveal their special abilities and weakness, in instruction, classroom management skills, etc. It is provides information for staff development.
11. *Indirect Measures:* Besides using the aforesaid methods, to know teacher enthusiasm, humour, judgement, objectivity, and puntuality can also be measured indirectly.

## Conclusion

Teacher education is a programme that is related to the development of teacher proficiency and competence that would enable and empower the teacher to meet the requirements of the profession and face the challenges therein. To know how far teacher is developing proficiency, competencies and empower themselves with changing needs of present society.

Aforementioned evaluation techniques help in evaluating teacher education and also to maintain quality in teacher education.

## REFERENCES

Atkins, A. (1996). *Teachers' Opinions of the Teacher Evaluation Process.* ERIC Identifier ED398628.

Bonfadini, J. (1998). "Should Students Evaluate their Teachers?", *Rural Living*, *52*(10): 40-41.

Brandt, R. (1996). "On a New Direction for Teacher Evaluation: A Conversation with Tom McGreal". *Educational Leadership*, *53*(6): pp. 30-33.

Cronbach, L.J. (1960). *Essentials of Psychological Testing* (2nd edn.). New York: Harper.

Danielson, C. (1996). *Enhancing Professional Practice a Framework for Teaching*. Alexandria, VA: Association or the Supervision and Curriculum Development.

Danielson, C. & McGreal, T. (2000). *Teacher Evaluation: To Enhance Professional Practice*. Alexandria. VA: Association for the Supervision and Curriculum Development.

Egelson, P. (1994, April). "Collaboration at Richland School District Two: Teachers and Administrators Design and Implement a Teacher Evaluation System That Supports Professional Growth." Paper presented at the Annual Meeting of the American Educational Research Association, New Orleans, LA. (ERIC Document Reproduction Service No. ED 376 159).

Lengeling, M. (1996). "The Complexities of Evaluating Teachers." (ERIC Document Reproduction Service No. ED 399 822).

Shulman, L. (1988). "A Union of Insufficiencies: Strategies for Teacher Assessment in a Period of Educational Reform". *Educational Leadership*, *46*(3): 36-41.

Strobbe, C. (1993). "Professional Partnerships". *Educational Leadership*, *51*(42): 40-41.

Typer, R.W. (1950). *Basic Principles of Curriculum and Instruction*. Chicago: University of Chicago Press.

Williams, W. & Ceci, S. (1997), "How am I Doing?". *Change*, 29(5): 12-23.

# 22

# Philosophy Education and Ethics/Values or Axiology

*Shiva Nath Prasad*

The key theme of the present book lies in the conceptual analysis of the three terms. In my title of this paper, I have intentionally not used "a comma" between the first word, i.e., philosophy and the second word "education"; as it is customary, not to use comma, etc. in the title. But I have used a conjunctival "and" before value/ethics; because, it is this conjunctive word, which commonly binds with some heavy meaning between the two different disciplines, into a common bond of unity, cohesion and harmony and values of life, which alone can make life successful and fruitful, to be termed as most congenial, and worth of high jewels of goodness and provide unthought of glories; tiding over the crises of life once for all. Symbolically, I have used the word "philosophy" at the first place, for what I may say, as a weakness on my part, as a student of philosophy, the other disciplines or subject of study, would seem somewhat secondary, this I may call my weakness. The next word "education" I wish to link with philosophy, my purpose is to make a comparative study of philosophy and education, in addition, to cover the philosophy of education. This stage is really going to the denser aspects of the two subjects of discourse, in the thick and thin. The last word "Ethics/value" is the word that is commonly applied, as applied domain or practical side of the theory matured and materialized as good philosophy, good education for a perfected life, that comes at a mature age; when one's reflections rises higher and highest to absolutely perfected life of divinity. This is the end state, or a stage of writing, to a point of ending or concluding as it is called in literature as "end note"/epilogue, etc. Symbolically, spot-lighting the word "philosophy"—may be called introducing "education" being the main thesis, and the last word "value/ethics" is the final conclusion. It may be said, while introducing any subject, the speaker has to be cordial, polite, impressive, encouraging; while the second stage is at the thick and thin of information, regarding the heart of the matter or the main theme; while the phase of ending is a state of throwing the gauntlet and hastily or even haphazardly or to indifferent mood, trying to get relieved of all these responsibilities and be relaxed.

In his book, he has dwelt upon "philosophy", specially saying that there is no one philosophy; but there are various types of philosophies, each having some characteristics of its own, which are specific to that individual philosophy, with its own aims and goals. He suggests people to know more and more of many philosophies, and subjects, in order to make a comparative study and it is for this reason, one benefits very heavily by reading the history of philosophies or even of other more of subjects of one's interests. For the study of any subject, one has to be able to know and understand the methods of the subjects' study, which comprises an important supplement of contemporary schools of thought which provides logical completion of the study in historical perspective.

He also says that the significant virtue of comparative study, really encourages thorough and honest investigation. Too often thoroughness is or may be "inhibited by the dominance of a prevailing point of view commonly, the teaching definitely favours the viewpoint of the instructor without there being any acknowledgement. Sometimes, the prevailing philosophy is openly indoctrinated; so the pertinent questions here arises is—can or does it count for an investigation in true sense. Is it not rather a limitation of inquiry, which precludes the asking of honest questions and seeking of honest answers? In this context, it may have to be inquired if it is not possible for a teacher to be so free from common prejudice as to conduct an honest investigation of the problems of philosophy, after having fully considering each viewpoint for what it is worth, and at the same time, openly acknowledging his own loyalty. Such teaching may not be common. It may be said, surely if the truth is truth, it must be capable of withstanding all the investigation that can be directed against it. It may often be, that truth can fully be believed and appreciated only to the extent that it is questioned and examined as Butler trias to stress.

Butler also mentioned another advantage of comparative approach that may become necessary method in teaching and studying philosophy. According to Butler, it is not enough for the student today to become schooled in a general accepted viewpoint just because it has become the spirit of the times. If he is to be given the opportunity for considering openly the problems of philosophy and their different attempted solutions, it means he must study all of the philosophies. It means also that his own viewpoint shall be assumed in the light of all the possible viewpoints, and that he shall find his own position on the basis of his own preference of that viewpoint to all of others. This is way of considered judgement which necessarily involves choice between alternatives, the way of true learning in which the tensions of thought awaken the student to responsible decisions (Butler: 35). In the Indian Texts—there are three terms in educative process—*śravana, manana, nididhyāsana.*

But Butler also plainly speaks about some of the limitations of the comparative approach which is subject to be supplemented by history of philosophy and also by other methods, depending on the particular school of or types of philosophical system with their different methods of idealism, realism, pragmatism, etc., but without proper approach, trying to make comparative study, would amount to mere game, but comparative study may be used as an instrument of classification, this is not to put it to a very good use, certainly not the best one. Its chief value lies in giving the student a broad perspective in which significant reflective insights can be awakened (Butler: 35-36).

In the context of definition of the word "secularism" Bertrand Russell had contended that there are words about which it has been said "to be definable", also there are words about which it is said "it is not definable", though it is also said that one knows and understands it, but cannot make out a precise definition, and one such word is "secularism".

In the similar vein, Butler says that it is difficult to define the word "education" but he does not stop only at this, he goes on enthusiastically, which is most uncommon, when he opines thus "even without implying an educational philosophy", an "evidence of the intimate relation between philosophy and education". In this way philosophy is most "indispensable from education" (p. 10). Butler further mentions that it is interesting to refer to John Dewey, who simply defines philosophy as "a general theory of education" (*Democracy and Education*, NY: MacMillan Company, 1916: 383). But many other philosophers feel that it is more than this, so Butler holds.

But if education is quite "undefinable", then can it also be "indescribable". No, the answer is, it is describable. So to make room for the most varieties of educational theory in a somewhat different way

> "as an activity or endeavour in which the more mature of human society deal with the less mature, in order to achieve greater maturity in them and contributes thereby to the improvement of human life" (Butler: 10).

Butler has made a differentiation between philosophy and education thus—(i) Philosophy is theoretical and speculative; education is practical. (ii) Philosophy asks questions, examining factors' of reality and experience, many of which are involved in the educative process; whereas the actual process of educating is a matter of actively dealing with these factors, i.e., teaching, organizing programmes, administering organizations, building curricula, etc.

As regards the relation between philosophy and education, Butler holds, there are two ways chiefly, (i) Philosophy yields a comprehensive understanding of reality, a world view, which when applied to educational practice, lends direction and methodology which are likely to be lacking otherwise. By way of reciprocation (ii) the experience of the education in nurturing the young, places him in touch with phases of reality which are considered in making philosophic judgements. Because of this, those who are actively engaged in educating can advise philosophers about certain matters of fact. That is to say, while philosophy is a guide, to education practice; education as the field of investigation yields certain data as a basis for philosophic judgements (Butler: 11).

Butler has deeply delved in regard to philosophy-education relations and has given many more points worth mentioning for greater knowledge of the reader/scholars. Butler says the relation between philosophy and education is quite enduring and also unending to deal with in a minor discussion within the limits of few pages. It may be admitted that, the science of education yields to the philosopher for further use in intimate association with children, young people and adults as students. This close association is unusual opportunity for observing nature as it is. A teacher can scarcely avoid formation of some attributes to the nature of man, as he is beheld in the pupil. It may asked, Is the human individual a mechanism of nature, an organism, a segment of society or a spirit? The educator may not venture the answer, but he can at least offer the philosopher some solid observations on which to base his conception of man, contends Butler.

Butler in this context of relation between philosophy and education poses a question—what are some of the problems philosophy investigates, which have a direct equivalents in educational policies? For this question, he advances three points:

(1) It is held that most philosophers are concerned with the nature of self. In this regard, certain questions may be asked, like the following—Is the self-physical, social or spiritual unit? Butler says, whatever the answer will be given by anyone, will go far in determining a person's attitude towards the pupil, in case education is one of his major interests or if the self is physical unity, then pupils are biological organisms. If it is spiritual unity, then pupils are souls with destinies which outreach both biological and social processes—replies Butler.

(2) Not only philosophy is heavily concerned with values, but education cannot afford to neglect values, rather, it must necessarily deal with values, even more than most of the social institutions. Philosophy asks some questions, like—What kind of existence do values have? How does man possess or realise values? Must efforts be put forward in this process? Or do values come to us without efforts like an inheritance? And Butler says such questions are relevant to education simultaneously. This can be explained with an example. It is true that a certain amount of effort is involved in the possession of value, this is just another way of saying that experiences which educate are fundamental

to any progress in experiencing or realizing value. Philosophically looked, educative activities as a means in the important life-task of leaving off the old and entering into the new which is more to be valued than the old (Butler: 11).

Value thinking in philosophy is also related to education in another important way, opines Butler, what is most important is the fact that education must have some objectives, if it is to be effective, otherwise it descends to the level of aimless activity which is anti-thesis of educative experience. But here a question can be raised, how can education have valid objectives unless these are formulated within the context of responsible thinking about value in general? So Butler contends, that there are so little awareness between value theory and educational objectives, and much superficial talk about objectives does not go far in perceiving this connection (*Ibid.*: 12).

(3) Butler thinks, whatever interest in philosophers asking questions and answers put forward, can scarcely stop before determining what his philosophizing implies for the educational process itself. He carries forward the matter, if the pupil is biological unit only, and the context within which objectives are set in purely naturalistic way, then the process of educating natural process, in no sense can be transcending the natural order. But if the pupil is spiritual being, and the objectives of education are anchored in immortality and an ultimate divine society, then the process by which man is educated must be consistently and carefully refined, so that personality is always treated as personality, never as mechanism, or near personality and so that societies inhibiting them in reaching out toward the ultimate (Butler: 12).

It may be added here, that in all connections between philosophy and education, the certainly of transfer is by no means assured. An educator may enjoy theorising and not put into performance or practice, out of the choice of the individual. Theorising merely cannot assure any result without practice. Theory without practice is a half-way process. Both theory and practice are essential. No theory is fully express until it s expressed in practice. Theory and practice both are like two sides of the same coin.

The relation between philosophy and education may be interpreted in another way, by noting that philosophy consists of three essential branches, e.g., epistemology, metaphysics and ethics, so do we have similar branches in the case of education. There is no such parallel. But according to Butler, educational philosophy contains four parts, i.e., education is a (1) social process, (2) pupil is the other central aspect, (3) objectives of education, and (4) education as process.

To my mind, the relation between the two can best be most simplistically expressed with a small cut sentence—"Philosophy is to education, what is metaphysics and epistemology is to education". That is, philosophy "as a study to know the reality", so far this, "it is a theory of metaphysics", and to know by what process about reality is metaphysics. Philosophy provides metaphysics and education, the way of knowing, i.e., epistemology. This can be further more elaborated for a more meaningful interpretation.

It is contended that philosophy of education is concerned with the following facts:

(i) developing as a coherent educational philosophy, it helps the educator develop a clear understanding of our own values and beliefs about education which can guide their teaching principles.

(ii) Evaluating educational practice—by examining underlying philosophical assumptions of different approaches, educator can make more informed decisions about curriculum, pedagogy, and assessment.

(iii) Promoting meaningful dialogue about education—It provides a framework for discussing and debating fundamental questions about nature of education.

(iv) Fostering a more just and equitable education—by critically examining the social and political dimensions of education. Philosophy and education can help educator work towards creating a more inclusive and empowering learning environment for all students.

Several other questions in regard to relation also are posed which indicate that the two are intricately linked and philosophy provides foundational framework for teaching methods, conversely the educational services as practical means for realizing and transmitting through general philosophy informs education and educational underlies philosophical problems. Some questions also arise about how philosophy influences setting aims and objectives and a philosophy of life values, shapes goals and objectives of education curriculum, teaching and shaping education are another objectives of education.

There are some scholars who classify philosophies as of "seven types" as follows:

(1) *Essentialism*—It focuses on transmitting essential knowledge and skill through a structured curriculum, emphasizing traditional academic disciplines.

(2) *Progressivism*—It emphasizes learning through experience, problem and solving and active engagement with a focus on adapting to change and developing critical thinking.

(3) *Perennialism*—It is about values. Knowledge that transcends time and culture, focusing on enduring ideas and principles found in the classic works of literature and philosophy.

(4) *Existentialism*—It emphasizes individual freedom, responsibility and self-discovery encouraging students to find their own meaning and purpose in life.
(5) *Behaviourism*—It focuses on observable behaviour and uses techniques like positive and negative reinforcement to shape student action.
(6) *Linguistic Philosophy*—It emphasizes the importance of language and communication in learning and understanding, focusing on developing clear and effective communicating skill.
(7) *Constructivism*—It views learning as an active process where individuals construct their own understanding of the world based on their experiences and interactions. A chart with the categories. Traditional and contemporary may clarify the positions.

The educationist and the educationists have tried to the interpretation "of what education owes to philosophy".

Though Butler's book notes "Four Philosophies", but it speaks of six philosophies, and starts with the naturalistic philosophy, which perhaps no other scholar has tried to study and develop deep; the other are realism, idealism, pragmatism and existentialism, with a combine to five, instead of four, but besides these five, he adds, a sixth one discipline "Language Philosophy", so that the contemporary philosophy is not divorced from its high prestige.

The question as to how education influences philosophy still remains to be explained. Butler mentions that there are four pillars of education. While dwelling upon educational aspects, "he gives first position to social aspect of education". Since, man is the first primary unit of society, so it is said that there is sociological basis of education, apart from philosophical, biological, psychological, economic basis of education, which is the reservoir of information in educational discussion, creating enormous information. To see the real picture of reciprocal influence can be seen in the triangle mode, or rectangular but the most visually through colour lens of prism as having multi-colour hues.

The way of philosopher's influences on education and vice versa, can be explained in the light of the following hint-points—(i) dynamic application, (ii) transmission of knowledge, (iii) generating new philosophical principles, (iv) philosophy prescribe the goals and essentials of good life. It means value-laden life with goodness, virtues and excellence, (v) philosophy deals wit the ends, education with means.

Butler very intelligently takes the matter of value in education; by not taking help of the books of ethics. He has done well to use a very expansive word, "axiology", to include four parts or aspects e.g., (i) Ethical Values, (ii) Aesthetic Values, (iii) Religious Values, and (iv) Social Values.

Butler contends that axiology is a great field of philosophy. We recognize that there are two different realms—realm of being and realm of values. While, admitting the existence aspects of things, is one fact, while entering into our experience is important, but it cannot also be denied, that our experience are made of values and worth, which is somehow attached to these things.

It is granted that we live in this world, but we, our works, acts, do, must of our living at the level of choosing, desiring and preferring. Though roots of our axiology are found in Plato, Aristotle, St. Thomas and Spinoza, etc. "Axiology" is a theory of value and it is a young child in the family of philosophy.

Ethics is the theory of moral good, is one of the oldest fields of philosophy.

Aesthetic is the theory of beauty and has a long history. The word "axiology", stems from "axio", which means "of like value" or "worth as much as".

There are different types of values or different theories of values. Ethical values. It is possible to consider the ethical values under two categories—immediate and ultimate. If we do not have belief in God, we do not see any values in religious beliefs.

Butler has too much influence on social values, much more in education which can transmute the dross into gold in terms of value. Butler gives some examples of social values, which has wide appeal, for reasons beyond our grasp.

(1) There is sheer orderliness and dependability in social structures, for to be preferred to the chaos which must have preceded civilization which now erupts like a volcano, amid the changing fortunes of war, while control is passing from one side to the other.
(2) Another is democracy or the effective participation of individuals in setting the direction wholly determined by someone else.
(3) Then there is value of a united front and the strength it affords in fighting such common enemies of human welfare as hunger, poverty, crime, disease and war.
(4) To add as an example of word peace that orderliness and dependability of social structure on the worldwide scale embracing all mankind, which does not primitive chaos.

It is essential to note, Butler is not only concerned with "general philosophy but also applied philosophy and education". In this regard four points are essential—(1) Education as institution, (2) The pupil, (3) Objectives of education, (4) Educative processes. The seriatim shows the first preference to social institution which is equally applicable to both philosophy and ethics.

Having said the above, it is the prime time or the right time to pause for a moment, rethink and correlate philosophy, education into union with a message of ultimate values as well as immediate values, as it were, the two wings of a bird. The most ancient texts of the Vedas, the Upaniṣads, the Brāhmaṇa Granthas, the Purāṇas, the Śrutis, the Smṛtis, the great epics of *Rāmāyaṇa*, *Mahābhārata*, the Nīti Granthas; which were taught in forests and the *gurukula*s, which were then the institutions of learning, as an old educational systems interested with the super most values, which worked to make life flowered into blessedness with value-laden life, with gifts and bounties and grandeurs, owing to embededness of good qualities like to tell the truth, do not lie, don't kill, live a friendly, harmonious life, run by religious commands of the religions texts, etc., which are at once a philosophy, education, science, art any and every field, whether theoretical or practical, philosophy or education as theory compounded with values means a heaven descended on earth, even Divinity descended as a common man, to teach, preach as precept and practice.

We are living in a civilized world, as homo sapiens, having accepted the "evolutionary theories—like survival of the fittest, struggle for existence", but are not "the struggles" and warring tendencies, signs, of the savage or brute society? Even when once civilized, why are we forced to adopt the life of the savages. Is it or may it be called a truly civilized way of life? We have craze of Greek society, at the apex of the world. Aristotle called man as "rational animal", should we feel happy or sorry for name of "animal" with man. It does not sound well and good. The Indian Śastras cannot accept such epithets, rather man is called *amṛtasya putrāḥ*, the child of immortality. To be immortal, one has to embibe and embellish life with immortal or perennial virtues and excellence. We have to adopt those by adequate education as means to become a perfected personality with a good citizenry, justness, fellow feeling, friendliness, non-injury, non-harming, and live peaceably with all, as all, being as it were, one common-humanity, the word humanity can be scanned as "human+unity", or "common+unity" for community. We should at once realize, all the arts, sciences, philosophy, education are meant to bring a "best possible world", and all must join this mission. This is the crux of a peaceful, purposeful life in entirety. Philosophy and education can do miracles, if we make efforts. Nature poet asks, "what man has made of Man, except enmities and angularities, thorns to prick to bleed". So the lesson is—"One impulse from vernal wood, can teach us more of Man, Of moral evils and of good, Than All Sages can". It means, Nature is equal for all, it does not distinguish anyone, anything. So the better guide is Nature. God created man and women as equal, but they acted mischievously. Shakespeare calls man "a paragon of animal" or arch animal, owing to their self-chosen bad acts. So, Man can realize, awaken and adopt values/virtues by resolute will. Man is himself good for himself, or evil for himself. He alone is responsible for either good or evil, as it is said, man is both friend and foe of himself; he is responsible for liberation or bondage, through his acts. He is himself liberator. Let him do acts for liberation, not for bondage. It needs education for good acts, that are liberating. Man can reach to Divinity by his own acts. The Gītā gives ample lessons for refinement of life.

# Index